FLESH AND BLOOD

Philip Osment

**Published by Methuen Drama in association
with Method & Madness**

A Methuen Fast Track Playscript

First published in Great Britain in 1996
by Methuen Drama
an imprint of Reed International Books Ltd
Michelin House, 81 Fulham Road, London SW3 6RB
and Auckland, Melbourne, Singapore and Toronto
in association with Method & Madness
25 Short Street, London SE1 8LJ
and distributed in the United States of America
by Heinemann, a division of Reed Elsevier Inc.
361 Hanover Street, Portsmouth, New Hampshire
NH 03801 3959

ISBN 0 413 71020 3

A CIP catalogue record for this book is available from the
British Library

Typeset by Wilmaset Ltd, Birkenhead, Wirral
Printed in Great Britain by Cox & Wyman Ltd, Reading,
Berkshire

Caution

Method & Madness

present the world premiere of

FLESH AND BLOOD

by Philip Osment

First performance at the Northcott Theatre, Exeter,
on 10 April 1996.

Method & Madness

Artistic Director
Mike Alfreds
Executive Director
James Williams
Executive Assistant
Mei Chapman
Design Associate
Paul Dart
Accountancy Services
Robert Smith ACIS
Administrative Assistant
Lesley Rowlings
Production Manager
Sacha Milroy
Costume Supervisor
Jill Pennington
Marketing and Press Manager
Margred Pryce
Tour Marketing Services
The Magenta Partnership 0171–735 2835
National Press Representative
Sharon Kean Associates 0171–254 6489

Directors
Stephen Remington
  (Chairman)
John Welch
  (Deputy Chairman)
Lynda Farran
Elizabeth Gard
Jenny Harris
Dr Christopher Johnson
Siobhan McCarthy
William Wilkinson
Pam Ferris
Mel Kenyon

Keep in touch ...
Please let us know what you think about our work – your
feedback is invaluable. To hear about the latest
developments in our repertoire and for touring information,
simply send your name and address (no stamp needed) to:
Marketing Department, Method & Madness
FREEPOST (Lon 1033), London SE1 8YY

Cambridge Theatre Company trading as Method &
Madness Reg. Charity no 259263

Method & Madness

> **Method & Madness** believes that the essential nature of theatre is its immediacy, that every performance is a unique event and what is most important is the life that flows between the actors and the audience. Theatre should be an adventure and a celebration of that life.

For our first season, we have brought together a permanent team of actors, designers, technicians and a writer to create a repertoire of three productions – *Jude the Obscure*, *Private Lives* and *Flesh and Blood*, all directed by Mike Alfreds and designed by Paul Dart – an artistic partnership celebrated for excellent productions including *Les Enfants du Paradis*, *A Handful of Dust* and *Emma*.

Working closely together over a long period, **Method & Madness** develops performances which have both the richness and skill of intensive preparation and the vitality and spontaneity of live theatre.

Method & Madness was formerly Cambridge Theatre Company

'One heck of a way to launch a new venture'
Manchester Evening News

Flesh and Blood completes a trilogy of plays written for Mike Alfreds all set in Devon where I grew up myself. The first play was about someone returning to Devon after many years; the second was about an eleven year old who will, one day leave; and this play is about people who are unable to escape.

Farmers and their families can lead very isolated lives; the business of farming is a way of life from which it is impossible to escape; often their whole family history is bound up with the farm; at the same time they are constantly dealing with life and death and usually have access to guns . . .

I feel that I have been circling ever closer to this material. The story has long held a strong fascination for me – maybe because of a certain claustrophobia I felt as a child.

Flesh and Blood was developed in consultation with Mike Alfreds. I would like to thank Lin Coghlan, Tony McBride, Maxine Bracher and Mrs H.N. Osment for their helpful comments and most particularly Nina Ward for all her support and advice.

Philip Osment

Flesh and Blood
by Philip Osment

Rose	Geraldine Alexander
Charles	Martin Marquez
William	Simon Robson
Shirley	Abigail Thaw
Director	Mike Alfreds
Costumes, Set &	
Lighting Designer	Paul Dart
Dialect Coach	Joan Washington
Voice Coach	Patsy Rodenburg
Sound Designer	Simon Whitehorn
Company Stage Manager	Jo Matheson
Deputy Stage Manager	Sid Charlton
Assistant Stage Manager	Tim Hughes
Technical Stage Manager	Faz Kemp
Wardrobe & Wigs Mistress	Helen Weatherburn
Set Construction	Scott Fleary Ltd
Transport Services	Southern Van Lines
Graphic Design	Oxygen
Production Photography	Simon Annand
Print Photography	David Scheinmann

The action takes place over a thirty-year period on a farm in Devon

There will be one interval
Running time: about 2 hours 30 mins

First performed at the Northcott Theatre, Exeter, on 10 April 1996. The production subsequently tours to Poole Arts Centre, Warwick Arts Centre, Oxford Playhouse and London's Lyric Theatre, Hammersmith.

Biographies

Geraldine Alexander (Rose)
Theatre: Star-gazey Pie & Sauerkraut (Royal Court); Blithe Spirit
(Theatre Royal, York); Miss Julie, A Doll's House (New End Theatre);
Count of Monte Cristo, An Inspector Calls, Hamlet (Royal Exchange);
All God's Chillun Got Wings (Leeds Playhouse); The Plain Dealer,
Richard III, The Master Builder (RSC); Twelfth Night, Jumping The
Rug (RSC/Almeida); Sweet Bird of Youth (West End). Television:
Vacillations of Poppy Carew, Perfect Scoundrels, Rumpole, Poirot,
Hannay, Bust, Victoria Wood Christmas Show, Casualty, Miss
Marple, A Very Peculiar Practice, The Gay Lord Quex (BBC). Film:
Méchant Garçon.

Martin Marquez (Charles)
Theatre: Uncle Silas, The Revenger's Tragedy (Cambridge Theatre
Company); Hamlet, A View From The Bridge, Once In A While The
Odd Thing Happens, The Slicing Edge, Road, High Society (Wolsey
Theatre, Ipswich); Biloxi Blues (Library, Manchester); Romeo and
Juliet (Nottingham Playhouse); Royal Hunt of The Sun (Compass
Theatre); Kathy and the Hippopotamus (Greenwich Studio); Legends
of Evil (Altered States); Macbeth (Orchard Theatre Company).
Television: The Bill, In Suspicious Circumstances (ITV); Desmonds
(Channel 4).

Simon Robson (William)
Theatre: Amphitryon (Gate Theatre); The Danube, Mill On The
Floss (Shared Experience); Long Day's Journey Into Night
(Cambridge Theatre Company); Eurovision (Kevin Wallace
Productions); A Midsummer Night's Dream (Salisbury Playhouse).
Television: The Bill, Faith (ITV); Fair Game (BBC). Radio: Death
and the Kings Horseman (Radio 3).

Abigail Thaw (Shirley)
Theatre: Don't Know Where, Don't Know When, Her Infinite
Variety, Mary Wollstonecraft – A Life (Dangerous Reputations Co. –
Conway Hall & tour); Brutality of Fact (New End, Hampstead);
Bloody Hero (BAC); A Midsummer Night's Dream (Theatre Royal,
York); Sweet Revenge (Bill Kenwright); Pride and Prejudice (Royal
Exchange, Manchester); Moscow Gold (RSC); The Importance of
Being Earnest, A Chorus of Disapproval, A View From The Bridge,
Noises Off, Of Mice and Men (Everyman Theatre, Cheltenham);
Cinders (Royal Court Theatre Upstairs). Television: Spywatch
(BBC); Pie In The Sky II, The Bill, White Girls on Dope (ITV).

Mike Alfreds (Director)
Artistic Director of **Method & Madness**.
Theatre: What I Did in The Holidays, Emma, Uncle Silas, A Handful of Dust, Les Enfants du Paradis (with David Glass), The Dearly Beloved, The Game of Love and Chance (with Neil Bartlett), The Revenger's Tragedy, The Country Wife, Lady Windermere's Fan (Cambridge Theatre Company); Arabian Nights Trilogy, Bleak House, Science Fictions, Cymbeline, The Merchant of Venice, The Seagull (Best Revival BTA/Drama Awards), La Ronde, A Handful of Dust, The Comedy Without a Title, False Admissions, Successful Strategies, Marriage, The Three Sisters, Too True to be Good (Shared Experience); The Cherry Orchard (Best Production BTA/Drama Awards, Plays and Players Award), The Wandering Jew, Countrymania (RNT), The Miser, The Seagull (Oxford Stage Company); Trouble in Paradise (Talking Pictures); A Flea in Her Ear (Theatr Clwyd/West Yorkshire Playhouse, nominated for TMA/Martini Award). Translations/adaptations: Jude the Obscure, Emma, Uncle Silas, Les Enfants du Paradis (with David Glass), Arabian Nights, Bleak House, The Seagull, Three Sisters, The Cherry Orchard, A Handful of Dust, La Ronde, The Comedy Without a Title, Marriage, Countrymania, The Miser, The Wandering Jew (with Michelene Wandor), Suitcase Packers. Work abroad: USA, Canada, Australia, New Zealand, Norway, Germany, Israel and China.

Paul Dart (Costumes, Set & Lighting Designer)
Design Associate, **Method & Madness**
Theatre: What I Did in The Holidays, Emma, Uncle Silas, A Handful of Dust, Les Enfants du Paradis, The Dearly Beloved, The Game of Love and Chance, The Revenger's Tragedy, The Country Wife, Lady Windermere's Fan (Cambridge Theatre Company); The Cherry Orchard, The Wandering Jew, Countrymania (RNT); One Thousand and One Nights (Theatre der Stadt Heidelberg); Arabiske Netter (Bergen National Theatre); Beauty and the Beast, Saturday Sunday Monday, When We Are Married, Peter Pan (Birmingham Rep). Retail design: Head of Design for Obsessions and James Glancy Designs.

Philip Osment (Writer)
Plays: Telling Tales, This Island's Mine (published in *Gay Sweatshop: Four Plays and a Company* ed. Philip Osment, Methuen); The Dearly Beloved, What I Did in The Holidays (both published by Samuel French Ltd), The Undertaking, Flesh and Blood. One Act Plays: Who's Breaking?, Listen, Sleeping Dogs.

Characters

Rose
William
Charles
Shirley

Setting: a farm in Devon

Note
This text went to press before the opening night and may
therefore differ from the version as performed.

Part One

Scene One

Rose *enters. She is dressed in mourning clothes. She hums a funeral hymn to herself. She goes to her father's photo on the wall and looks at it.*

William *enters. He is also dressed in mourning. He looks lost.*

Rose   You going to get changed?

William   Yeah.

He doesn't move.

Rose (*sings under her breath*)   Father in Thy gracious keeping
Leave we now Thy servant sleeping.

Charles *comes to the door also in mourning. He stands looking at them.*

Rose   Aunty Cissie looked old.

William   She is old.

Rose   She said to me, 'We're the only ones left now, Rose.'

William   Mmmmm.

Rose *takes off her hat.*

Rose   She was in a lot of pain with her arthritis. She said, 'I'm just waiting for my deliverance.'

William   Sad to end up like that. She hasn't got any money. Uncle Ted left her penniless. He spent money like water. Dad always said he'd end up bankrupt.

Rose   Remember when he wanted dad to buy that new milking parlour?

William   Yeah.

Rose   'Trouble with you, Teddy, your pockets aren't deep enough . . .'

Rose/William   '. . . and your arms are too long.'

They laugh.

Charles   And the trouble with dad was he was a mean old bugger.

Rose   Charlie!

Charles   It's true.

He starts to go.

William   That sow's about to farrow.

Charles   Tonight?

William   Looks like it.

Charles   Oh.

He looks at **Rose**.

Rose   I'll keep an eye on her.

William   It's his job.

Charles   I'm going out.

Rose   Tonight?

Charles   Yes, tonight.

Rose   Don't you want your tea?

Charles   No.

He goes.

William   Where's he going?

Rose   I don't know.

She calls up the stairs.

Your new shirt is on the bed.

William   What new shirt?

Rose   The one he bought himself for his birthday.

William *shakes his head. Pause.*

Rose   Your other trousers are down here. You want me to press them for you?

Charles (*off*)   You wannoo wipe my arse for me as well?

Rose *looks at* **William**. *She goes to the kitchen and comes back with the teapot and two teacups. She is humming the hymn again. She waits for the tea to brew.*

Rose   Nice of Mr Luscombe to come to the funeral.

William   Well, he's a neighbour.

Rose   There wasn't much love lost between dad and him. Remember when they nearly had a fight about who the hedge belonged to?

William   Yeah.

Rose   Dad threatened to set the dogs on him.

They both laugh.

William   And now dad's dead. Old Luscombe's won that battle.

Charles *returns in his shirt and long johns.*

Rose   When did you last change them?

Charles   They're clean.

Rose   You sure?

William   He idn going to be showing his pants to anyone tonight I hope. Are you, Charlie?

Rose (*handing him his trousers*)   Here. You sure you don't want me to press them?

Charles   No.

Rose   Won't take a minute.

Charles   Haven't got time.

William   What's the rush?

Charles   Mind your own business.

William   Your father's hardly been in his grave for two hours.

Charles   So?

William   You didn't ought to be going out tonight, boy.

Charles   You mind your own bloody business. You never want anybody to go out anywhere. Scared they're going to spend some money.

Rose   Charles.

Charles   I can do what I bloody well like.

Rose   Don't, Charles!

Charles   Am I suppose to sit at home being miserable with you two? Idn going to bring him back, is it?

They don't respond.

Makes me sick the way you two been going on all day. Bloody hypocrites. I'm not going to pretend that I loved that mean old bugger. I was glad to see him go. Maybe we can get on with our bloody lives now.

Rose   I wish you wouldn swear.

Charles   I'll bloody well swear as much as I bloody well like. I'm not going to ask no other bugger if I can bloody well swear. We can't all be as refined as you two. I didn't get sent to no private school, remember. Not like you and him.

Rose   You shouldn swear.

Charles   Arsehole, buggery, dick.

He goes.

William *shakes his head.*

Rose *pours* **William** *some tea.*

Rose   So cold in that churchyard.

William   He didn ought to be talking about dad like that.

He starts to cry.

Rose   Come on, now, Bill, that's not going to help anybody.

William   So few people at the funeral, Rose.

Rose   Don't be soft.

William   Not much to show for a life.

Rose He wouldn want us to be sitting here like this.

William So few people to mourn his passing.

A faint knocking.

Rose What was that?

William Your bloody cat drinking the milk, I expect.

Rose Snowy! Are you in that dairy again?

She goes.

William *crosses to the piano and tinkles the tune of 'The Ash Grove'.*

Rose (*in the kitchen*) Oh, hello, my dear, come in.

Shirley Mum sent me up with this.

Rose Oh, thank you. We're through here.

They enter the parlour.

Look what Shirley's brought, Bill.

She holds up a pie.

Shirley It's squab pie. Mother thought you might not have time to do any cooking what with the funeral and everything.

William That's very kind of you, Shirley.

Rose *makes a face at* **William** *behind* **Shirley**'s *back as if to express her incomprehension at* **Shirley**'s *mother's action.*

William Get another cup, Rose.

Rose Have that one. I'll get myself another.

Rose *goes with the pie.*

Awkward pause.

Shirley We just wanted to say how sorry we were.

William Yes. Yes.

Pause. In the kitchen **Rose** *is prising the pastry off the pie to look underneath.*

How are things down at the Red Lion?

Shirley All right.

William   Mr Webber's not working your mother too hard.

Shirley   She likes it.

William   You've been here quite a while now.

Shirley   Nearly three years. Mr Webber's talking about moving on though.

William   Is he?

Pause.

You and your mother going to come up and help us out turkey picking this year?

Shirley   Oh yes.

William   You were one of our best workers last year.

Shirley   I enjoyed it. It was the atmosphere. You know, everyone's excited about Christmas coming and they're earning a bit of extra money. And they're all laughing and joking. It's a real occasion. You know what I mean, Mr Thorne?

William   Yes, I do.

Shirley   I want to buy mum a blouse she was looking at in town so the money will come in handy. I love going out and getting the presents, wrapping them up. It's more fun giving the presents than getting them sometimes, idn it?

William (*entranced by her enthusiasm*)   Yes, I suppose it is.

Shirley   And I love decorating the tree. Do you have a tree?

William   We don't tend to go in for all that.

Shirley   Oh dear.

Rose *enters with another cup and pours herself some tea.*

Shirley   I've got to go home and get ready for the dance.

Rose   Dance tonight? Where?

Shirley   Village hall.

Rose   Not working behind the bar tonight, then?

Shirley   No. Not tonight.

Charles *enters*.

Charles   Rose!

Rose   What?

Charles (*changing his tone*)   Oh. Evening.

Shirley   Hello.

Rose   What do you want?

Charles   Nothing.

Rose   Shirley's mum has made us a lovely pie.

Charles   Oh.

Shirley   Right, well . . .

William   See you at the turkey picking.

Rose   Oh, yes.

Shirley   Thanks for the tea.

Rose *exits*. **Shirley** *follows. At the door she turns back.*

Shirley (*mouthed at* **Charles** *behind* **William***'s back*)   See
you later.

Charles *looks at* **William** *who hasn't seen*.

Shirley *goes*.

Pause. **Charles** *combs his hair*.

William   You get the tractor going?

Charles   Not yet.

William   Need to get the manure out.

Pause. They have nothing to say to each other.

Rose *returns with the pie*.

Rose   Here, look at this.

Charles   What?

Rose   Got hardly any meat in it. Bit of fatty mutton.

William   Very kind thought.

Charles (*quietly to* **Rose**)   You got any money?

Rose   How much you want?

William   Don't you go giving him money.

Charles   I only want ten bob.

William   You can't go out spending money all the time.

Charles   You mean bugger. You're just like the old man.

Rose   I saved a bit on the housekeeping this week.

William (*firmly*)   He's not having it and that's final.

Charles *stamps his foot.*

William   Now get on.

Charles *starts to go.* **Rose** *has taken a ten-shilling note out of her bag and slips it to him without* **William** *noticing.* **Charles** *goes.*

Rose   I'm going to give this to the dog.

William   Why?

Rose   Don't fancy it.

William   Why not?

Rose   You ever been in that kitchen down the pub?

He doesn't reply.

And you never know what might be in it.

William   What you mean?

Rose   You know who her family is?

William   Whose family?

Rose   Shirley's mother's brother is Curtis the gypsy. And their aunt's husband was that gyppo dad threw off our lower field that time.

William   You know I never follow it when you go on about who's related to who.

Rose   Well, anyway, Curtis is Shirley's uncle. Mrs Stephens, Shirley's mother, married a farm labourer from Plymouth way. But they got divorced. So then Mr Curtis got her the job housekeeping at the Red Lion. You know, after Mr Webber's wife ran off.

William (*not really interested*)   Oh.

Rose   Course you know what they say.

William   What about?

Rose   About Shirley's mother.

William   What?

Rose   That's she's more than just a housekeeper to Webber.

William   You don't know that, Rose.

Rose   The lipstick she wears.

Charles (*off*)   Bye.

Rose   Don't be late.

William   He's meant to be looking after those pigs.

Rose   All work and no play idn good for anybody.

William   He shouldn be going out tonight.

Rose   Won't do any harm.

William   This is just the start.

Rose   You leave him to me.

William   You encourage him.

Rose   I don't.

William   You always have.

Rose   You know what dad said to me before he died?

William   What?

Rose   'Keep the peace, Rose. Keep the peace.'

William *returns to tinkling on the piano.*

Rose   Dad loved that.

William   Mmmm.

William *plays the tune of 'The Ash Grove'.* **Rose** *hums along.*

Scene Two

The Ash Grove. Moonlight.

In the background **Rose** *and* **William** *can be heard singing.*

Charles   Come on.

Shirley   I'll ruin these shoes.

He laughs.

Shhh.

They listen.

Charles   That's Rose and William.

Shirley   They don't sound too sad.

Charles   Always playing music. Drives me mad. They
think they're so much cleverer and better than everybody
else. (*He mocks their singing by making the sound a dog will make at
music.*) Haooo hao hao haoooh.

Shirley   Don't.

They giggle. The music stops.

Rose (*off*)   Scamp!

Shirley *and* **Charles** *giggle.*

Rose (*off*)   Scamp! Quiet!

Charles   She's gone.

Shirley   It's a bit spooky here.

Charles   This is where you came picking bluebells that
time. Remember?

Shirley   Yes. That was in broad daylight.

Charles   I was chopping down a tree and I saw you
standing there. Like a fairy.

Shirley   We'd only just moved here. I wanted something to
brighten up our bedroom.

Charles   Always been my job to keep this wood clear. It's where the logs you use down at the pub come from. Good wood for burning, ash.

Shirley *shivers*.

Charles   You cold?

Shirley   Bit.

Charles   I've got a little hidey-hole over there.

Shirley   Oh yes?

Charles   Yes. It's a hollow tree trunk. I go in there when it rains sometimes. Nice and cosy.

Shirley   Mum says we need another load of logs.

Charles   I'll bring them down.

Pause.

Shirley   What was that?

Charles   Just the rooks.

Shirley   Give me a fright.

He impersonates the rooks.

Charles   Got a rookery over in them elms. Every winter all the crows and rooks from miles around come to roost there. Bloody pests really. Still, you mustn't get rid of a rookery.

Shirley   Why not?

Charles   Bad luck. If rooks desert the rookery it means the heir of the house is going to die. They can foretell doom, rooks.

Shirley   Don't!

He laughs.

Charles   I'll have to come out and just shoot a few of em.

Shirley   You superstitious?

Charles   No.

Shirley   Mum's always going on about things like that.
She saw a wren on the window-sill last week and said, 'He's
come to tell us somebody's going to die.'

Charles   And somebody did die.

Shirley   Oh yes!

Charles   Ooooohooooo.

Shirley   Don't, Charles.

Charles   Are you there, Dad?

Shirley   Stop it!

Charles   She was reading palms last night in the pub, your
mum.

Shirley   I know.

Charles   Can you do it?

Shirley *shrugs*.

Charles (*holding his hand out*)   Read mine. Tell me what our
future's gonna be like.

Shirley   I don't believe in all that.

She kisses his hand.

Charles   Yesterday I was standing in my little hidey-hole
watching the rain. And I closed me eyes and imagined that
you were in there with me.

Shirley   Did you now?

Charles   Yes. Just you and me in the root of a tree! Safe,
see. That's what it'll be like when we get our own place.

Shirley   Yes?

Charles   Yes. No Rose or William coming knocking on the
bedroom door telling me to get up. We'll be able to spend our
whole day in bed if we want to.

Shirley *laughs*.

Charles   We'll have a great big brass bed.

Shirley   Oh!

Charles   And loads of kids.

Shirley   You ever brought anybody else here? Like Mary Quick?

Charles   No.

Shirley   Not even Gwen Luscombe?

Charles   Can't remember.

Shirley   What did she used to be called?

Charles   Gwen Small.

Shirley   Mr Webber said she used to be sweet on you.

Charles   Don't know about that.

Shirley   You're much more handsome than Eddie Luscombe.

Charles   What about Tommy Youings?

Shirley   What about him?

Charles   Am I more handsome than him too?

Shirley   Course you are.

She kisses him.

Charles   Sometimes I used to go out with Gwen and I'd only have sixpence in my pocket. Dad never let us have any money if he could help it. (*To the air.*) You won't stop me this time, will you, old man? You bloody bastard.

Shirley   Charles!

Charles   What?

Shirley   He's only just died.

Charles   I wadn sorry to see him go.

Shirley   That's terrible.

Charles   The way he treated us. Like his slaves. We could never have anything when we were kids. Not even a bloody pet. I had a puppy once. He drowned it. I had hamsters, he sold them. He killed mother with overwork. No one knew what he was really like. Vicious bugger. I hated him.

Pause.

Shirley   I miss my dad.

Charles   Don't you ever see him?

Shirley   No.

They listen to the music.

Didn they ever want to get married?

Charles   Who?

Shirley   Rose and William.

Charles   Who'd have em?

They laugh.

They wouldn know what to do.

They laugh more.

Shirley   Your brother.

Charles   What about him?

Shirley   The way he stares.

Charles   Perhaps he's sweet on you.

They laugh.

Shirley   He's a lot older than you, isn't he?

Charles *impersonates* **William***'s stare.*

Shirley   Charles.

He carries on staring.

Isn't he?

He is still staring at her.

What are you doing? Stop it.

He carries on staring.

Don't. You're frightening me.

He moves towards her and puts his hands around her neck as if to strangle her. She screams. He holds her.

Shirley   He's a good piano player.

Charles   Should be. He had lessons at that school he got sent to.

Shirley   Why didn't you get sent away to school?

Charles   The old man didn wanna fork out the money.

Shirley   But he paid for William and Rose to go.

Charles   Mother made him. She was dead when it came to my turn.

Shirley   How old were you when she died?

Charles   Ten.

Shirley   Young.

Charles   Yeah. She had cancer.

Shirley   Oh.

Charles   You don't really understand at that age. I asked God if he'd let her live if I stopped having sweets or sugar in me tea.

Shirley   Awhhh.

She holds him maternally.

Good job you had Rose.

Charles   What you mean?

Shirley   Everyone says she dotes on you.

Charles *laughs dismissively.*

Charles   Can't wait to see their faces when I tell them. (*To the air.*) Shirley and me are getting married, Dad! What do you think of that?

Shirley   Shhhh.

Charles   They got to know sometime. There's a farm for sale over Weardon way.

Shirley   Yes?

Charles   Lower Kerscott.

Shirley   You do mean it, don't you, Charles?

Charles   Mean what?

Shirley   You're not just making it up.

Charles   Course I'm not.

Shirley   Sometimes . . .

Charles   What?

Shirley   It's like you live in a dream.

Charles   You sound like Rose. Nobody ever thinks I can do anything.

Shirley   I didn't mean that.

Charles   I'll bloody go and tell them now.

Shirley   No.

Charles   Why not?

Shirley   I don't want you to.

Charles   You don't want to be scared of them.

Shirley   No.

Charles   I'm going to get you a ring.

Shirley   Yes?

Charles   Yes.

He kisses her.

You want to see my hidey-hole?

Shirley   All right.

Charles   Will you show me your hidey-hole?

Shirley   Charles!

He kisses her.

Come on, then.

William *is playing 'Early One Morning'.*

Rose (*off*)   Oh, don't deceive me. Oh, never leave me.
     How could you treat a poor maiden so?

Scene Three

Early morning. The yard. **Rose** *is feeding the hens.*

Rose (*calling the hens to be fed*)   Here, cubby, cubby, cubby. Chick, chick, chick!

Charles *enters with his gun. He has two dead crows on strings.*

Rose   You going to see if you can get us a rabbit?

Charles   Could do.

Rose   I hope you're not going to hang those from any of the apple trees this time. They stink the orchard out. Cubby, cubby, cubby.

Charles   You going to town Thursday?

Rose   I wadn planning to.

Charles   Oh.

Rose   Why?

Charles   Wanted your help choosing a ring in Dobbs.

Rose   A ring?

Charles   Yes.

Rose   What sort of ring?

Charles   An engagement ring.

Rose   An engagement ring.

Charles   Yes.

Rose   This is a bit sudden. Who's it for?

Charles   Shirley Stephens.

Rose   Oh!

Charles   What?

Rose   I thought she was going out with the boy Youings.

Charles   Not any more.

Rose   You don't want to go rushing into anything, Charles.

Charles   I knew you'd be like this.

Rose   We've only just got the funeral over with.

Charles   So?

Rose   It's a big decision. I'm only thinking about what's best for you.

Charles   This is best for me. Shirley's best for me. I love her, Rose.

Rose (*to the hens*)   Come on, cubby, cubby, cubby.

Charles   I always thought this didn happen to us. That twadn something we were capable of. Mother and father never showed each other any affection, did they? Didn even sleep in the same room.

Rose   Don't know how you can talk about such things.

Charles   Did you ever see them touch each other?

Rose   They were brought up to be like that.

Charles   Don't know how they managed to do what they had to do to get us.

Rose   That's enough, Charles.

Charles   Just cause you never wanted to get married.

Rose   You don't know what you're talking about.

Charles   Well, why didn you marry that bloke from Seale Hayne College?

Rose   How could I? With mum just dead? What would dad have done? What would you and Bill have done? Somebody had to look after you. That's your trouble, you only think of yourself.

Charles   Is this enough for you, then?

Rose   Is what enough?

Charles   Living here with us?

Rose   You're my brothers.

Charles   Brothers, yeah. But there's some things you can't do with brothers, Rose.

Rose You've got a filthy mind, you know that? You're not natural.

Charles You're the one that's not natural.

Rose You can just stop it. How dare you!

Pause.

Charles Rosie, I want this more than anything I've ever wanted in my whole life.

Rose That hen's lame.

Charles I don't want to just live and die and never have any joy like the old man.

Rose The others'll start picking on it.

Charles Rose.

Rose What?

Charles Come to Dobbs with me.

Rose How are you going to afford to buy a ring?

Charles I've got that little bit of money mother left me.

Rose You're not supposed to touch that.

Charles Money's for spending.

Rose It'll be enough to buy a ring but it won't be enough to keep a wife.

Pause.

We ought to talk to Bill about it.

Charles Why?

Rose He ought to know.

Charles Bill can go hang himself.

Rose What are you going to do, Charlie, if you do get married? It's all very fine getting engaged.

Charles I thought you two could buy me out. Lower Kerscott's for sale.

Rose Charlie, you haven't thought this out. Bill would have to agree.

Charles   You could talk him round.

Rose   Don't know about that.

Charles   Look, I'm going to get that ring. Once we're engaged he'll have to like it or lump it.

Rose   Just give me a bit of time.

Charles   What for?

Rose   To bring him round.

Charles   I'm not going to keep her hanging on.

Rose   You could at least wait till after Christmas.

Charles   You come and help me choose the ring, I'll wait till Christmas.

Rose   I'll think about it.

He goes to touch her.

Now get off, Charles.

Charles   She's a lovely girl.

Rose   Mmmm.

Charles   You'd get on with her if you got to know her better.

Rose   Go and get that rabbit.

He goes.

Cubby, cubby, cubby.

Scene Four

The kitchen. **Charles** *is polishing his shoes and whistling just outside the door.*

William   Don't forget to ask in the butchers if they want some of our geese for Christmas.

Rose   I've got it down on my list.

William   And don't let them beat you down in price.

Rose   All right, all right.

William   I ought to come with you.

Rose   One of us'll have to stay home for the milking.

William   Charlie can do the milking.

Rose   He wants to go to town.

William   Don't know why.

Rose   I said he could.

William   Yes, well . . .

Rose   I didn't know you'd want to go.

William   I don't mind.

Rose (*whispers*)   He wants a little trip.

William   Don't let him go spending all his money.

Rose   We'll have to go again with the geese.

William   I know.

Rose   You and me could go then.

William   I told you, I don't mind.

Pause.

Don't know what's got into him lately.

Rose   What do you mean?

William   Listen to him.

They listen.

There's something going on.

Rose   I'll see what I can find out on our way into town. Probably just as well, you see?

William   What?

Rose   Might be easier for him to talk away from the farm.

William   Don't forget those nails.

Rose   They're on my list.

William   Have to make a bigger pen for those piglets.

Charles *enters.*

Charles   Us'll miss that bus if us dudn get going.

William   Don't forget to call in Curtis the gyppo's and see if he's got a dynamo for the tractor. He owes us for that scrap metal you let him take off us.

Charles   I'm not doing that.

William   Why not?

Charles   He dudn think he owes us anything. He thought if he came and collected it then he'd get it for nothing.

William   That wasn't what I arranged with him.

Charles   Well, I'm not doing it.

William   He knows he owes it to us.

Charles   We can buy a new dynamo. I'm not climbing around scrap-yards getting oil all over me best clothes.

William   Well, don't wear your best clothes.

Charles   I'll wear what I bloody well like.

Rose   Charlie!

Charles   He always has to interfere, dudn he?

William   What are you getting so mad about? Not scared of old Curtis, are you?

Charles   Don't be bloody stupid.

William   You shouldn't have let him take that metal without getting the money off him.

Charles   I told you he dudn think he owes us anything.

William   We won't be able to use the tractor.

Charles   Whenever you wanna go anywhere, there's always some errand he wants to send you on. Do your own bloody errands.

William   See how you like taking the manure out in the wheelbarrow.

Charles   It's my day off.

William   I never get a day off. I haven't had a day off for twenty years.

Charles   Oh, here we go. Tidn my fault you could never stick up to the old man. You should have told him to bugger off. But you were too much of a coward. Let him walk all over you.

William   If dad and me hadn't worked like we did we wouldn't have no farm. Then where would you be? You wouldn be going off to town dressed like a tailor's dummy for a start. You'd be working in some factory down Exeter.

Charles   Yeah and I'd have been a lot better off.

William   Well, there's the door.

Rose   Stop it.

William   Won't even go and take a dynamo off a tractor down Curtis's and then talks about working in a factory.

Charles   I'm not gettin it.

Rose   I'll go down Curtis's and see if he's got a dynamo.

William   Don't let him charge you.

Charles   That's all you think about.

William   Someone has to.

Charles   Come on, Rose.

William   I'll get the old one so you don't come back with the wrong model.

He goes.

Charles   I'll bloody swing for him one day.

Rose   It wouldn have hurt you.

Charles   What would he think?

Rose   Who?

Charles   Curtis.

Rose   What do you mean?

Charles   I told him he could have the scrap for free.

Rose Why did you do that?

Charles He had to come all the way out here.

Rose Cause of her?

Charles Who?

Rose Shirley.

Charles No.

Rose Just because she's Curtis's niece you don't have to let him walk all over you. Give em an inch and they'll take a mile.

Charles I want to ask Shirley over at Christmas.

Rose Oh.

Charles That all right?

Rose I suppose.

Charles You spoken to him yet?

Rose Patience, Charles.

Charles Come on then.

Rose I'm nearly ready.

Charles The jewellers closes one till two, you know.

Rose Just check I've got everything.

He goes. **Rose** *checks her list.*

William *returns with the dynamo wrapped up in paper.*

William What's wrong with him?

Rose Nothing.

William He doesn't know how easy he's had it. He never had the thrashings I had as a kid.

Rose Come on.

She holds out her bag. He puts it in.

Rose *goes.*

Scene Five

Christmas night. The parlour.

Rose, **William** *and* **Charles** *are playing Sevens.*

Rose *burps.*

Rose   Pardon. That's that Christmas pudding. Always gives me indigestion.

They continue playing.

Did you think that goose was a bit tough?

William   What you mean?

Rose   I thought it was.

William   It wadn tough.

Rose   What did you think, Charlie?

Charles   Eh?

Rose   Bout the goose.

Charles   What about it?

Rose   You think it was tough?

Charles   Bit.

William   Come on, play your cards.

Charles *plays a card.* **Rose** *plays.* **William** *plays.*

Rose (*to* **William**)   I wondered who had that. You've been holding that back, haven't you? Charles!

Charles   What?

Rose   Your turn.

Charles   Oh.

He plays a card.

Rose *plays a card.*

William *plays a card.*

Rose   That's another king he's got rid of.

Charles *plays a card.*

Rose   That's a diamond.

Charles   Eh?

Rose   You've put it on the hearts pile.

Charles   Oh.

He takes the card back and plays another.

Rose   Lovely service in church this morning.

She plays. **William** *plays.*

You should have come, Charles.

Charles   Won't get me in there.

Rose   Bill played the organ beautifully.

William   Mmmm.

Charles   Waste a time. Bloody church.

William   Don't be disrespectful now.

Charles *has played.*

Rose   I can't go.

William *plays.*

Charles   I can't go either.

William   You sure?

Charles   Course I'm bloody sure.

Rose *plays.* **William** *plays.*

Charles   I still can't go.

Rose   Neither can I.

William   One of you can.

Rose   It's not me.

Charles   Don't look at me. You always think it's me.

Rose   Have you got the eight of clubs?

Charles   No.

Rose   You sure?

Charles   Yes.

Rose   Might be behind one of your other cards.

William   He hadn got it.

Rose   So you're holding that back as well.

William   Somebody's got the jack of diamonds.

Rose   Tidn me.

They look at **Charles**.

Charles   The ten's not down, is it?

William   I put it down ages ago.

Charles   Oh.

He lays the jack of diamonds. The other two smile at each other.

I didn see you put it down.

Rose   You're not concentrating, Charlie.

William   You didn want to put it down, did you?

Charles   What you mean?

William   Only teasing.

Charles   I wadn bloody cheating.

Rose   He didn't say you were.

Charles   Bloody stupid game anyway.

William   Don't start sulking.

Charles   You can bloody well play by yourselves.

Charles *throws his cards down.*

Rose *and* **William** *look at each other.*

Charles   Callin me a cheat! I wadn cheating. I hadn't seen the bloody ten.

William   All right! All right! It's only a game.

Rose   Come on, I'll redeal.

Charles   No!

William   Don't be childish, Charlie.

Charles   I'm not bloody childish. Just shut up!

Rose   Shhh.

William   What?

Rose   Dog's barking.

Charles *and* **Rose** *look at each other.* **Charles** *gets up.*

William   Don't go out there kicking him.

Charles *mimes pouring drinks to* **Rose**. *She nods.* **Charles** *goes.*

William *sighs.*

William   He's enough to try the patience of a saint.

Rose   You going to give us a tune?

William   Not feeling like it, Rosie.

Pause.

Has he fed the pigs?

Rose   Don't think so?

William   Better go and do it.

Rose   Do you want a drink of port?

William   Port?

Rose   Yes.

William   Where did that come from?

Rose   Charlie bought it.

She gets out some glasses.

Charles *returns with* **Shirley**.

Charles   Look who's here.

Rose   Oh. Come in, my dear. Let her get near the fire, Bill.
You walked all the way up the lane? Must be freezing. There
you are. Sit down there.

Shirley   Thank you.

Rose   What a lovely dress.

Shirley   Christmas present.

Rose   From your mum.

Shirley   Sort of. Mr Webber really.

Rose   I see.

Charles   Want some port?

Shirley   Lovely.

He starts pouring the drinks.

Rose   I hear he's thinking of emigrating.

William   Who?

Rose   Mr Webber down the pub.

Charles   I didn't know that.

Shirley   Yes.

Charles   Here we are then.

He hands out the drinks.

Shirley   Happy Christmas.

Will/Charles/Rose   Happy Christmas.

Shirley   I've brought you these.

Rose   Oh, thank you. Look, Bill.

William   Very nice.

Charles   Aren't you going to open it?

She does so.

Shirley   And I thought you might like this, Mr Thorne.

William   Oh.

She hands him a parcel.

Rose   You shouldn't have gone to all this trouble, Shirley.

Shirley   Twadn any trouble. Here.

She gives **Charles** *a present.*

Rose   Chocolates. Mmm. What have you got, Bill?

William (*holding up a songbook*)   Popular songs.

Rose   Oh, very nice.

William *laughs.*

William   Well I never.

Charles *has opened his present. It is a tie.*

Charles   Thank you.

Rose   Very nice. It will go with your new shirt.

Charles   Hang on.

He goes.

Rose   It's like Father Christmas coming, idn it, Bill?

William   Yes it is. (*He laughs.*) Goodness!

Rose   You want a chocolate?

William   Oh.

Rose   Don't take all day.

William *takes a chocolate.*

Rose   Shirley.

Shirley   They're for you.

Rose   Go on.

Shirley *takes one.*

Rose   Mmmm.

Silence.

Your mother all right?

Shirley   Yes, thank you. She said the goose was lovely.

Rose   That's good. Didn't see you at church this morning.

Shirley   We had a late night in the pub last night.

Rose   Lovely service. Saw Mrs Youings.

Shirley   Oh yes.

Rose   She hadn heard from Tommy.

Shirley   No?

Rose   Funny him just going off like that, isn't it?

Shirley   Yes.

William   Where's he gone?

Rose   Looking for work up the country, I think.

Pause.

Nice chocolates.

Pause.

Charles *returns. He has put on his new shirt and the tie.*

Charles   There.

Rose   Very smart.

William *is looking at the songbook.*

Charles   Going to give us a tune, Bill?

William   All right then.

Rose *goes to the piano.*

Rose   We usually have carols Christmas night. Here, Bill.

She gets out a music book.

Our mother used to sing this one, Shirley. 'The Cherry Tree',
do you know it?

Charles (*sings*)   Mary got cherries
         By one two and three.

William   That's the last verse.

Rose   It's the wrong key as well. He's tone deaf, Shirley.

William *starts playing.*

William   Come on, Rose.

Rose   Joseph was an old man
         An old man was he,
         He married with Mary
         The Queen of Glory.

William   Joseph took Mary
         Into the orchard wood
         Where there was apples, plums, cherries
         As red as any blood.

Rose   Then bespoke Mary
         So meek and so mild:

    Get me some cherries, Joseph
    For my body's bound with child.

Shirley   It's lovely.

Charles   More port.

Shirley   All right.

William   Then bespoke Joseph
    These words so unkind:
    Let them get you cherries, Mary
    That did your body bind.

Charles   Mean old bugger.

William   Then bespake Jesus
    All in his mother's womb:
    The highest bough of the cherry tree
    Shall bow down to Mary's knee.

William/Rose   Mary got cherries
    By one, two and three,

Charles *joins in*.

    Mary got cherries
    For her young son and she.

Shirley *claps*.

Shirley   You're a very musical family.

Rose   William's the musician. He could have gone to music college, Shirley.

Shirley   Really?

Rose   Had a scholarship and everything.

William   I didn have a scholarship.

Rose   You did.

William   The teacher said I stood a good chance of getting one.

Rose   There you are then.

Shirley   Mum used to send me to dance classes when I was small.

Rose   Oh yes?

Shirley   I always said I was going to be a dancer.

Rose   Oh.

Pause.

Shirley   What a lovely brooch.

Charles   Ahhhhhh.

Shirley   What?

Charles   She only ever puts that on at Christmas.

Shirley   It's beautiful.

Charles (*whispers*)   Her fiancé gave it to her.

Rose *laughs.*

Rose   Honestly, Charles.

Charles   Oh, she's going red. Didn know you still blushed, Rosie.

Rose   Don't listen to him, Shirley.

Shirley   I won't.

Rose   Someone I knew at Seale Hayne gave it me.

Charles   Oh Danny Boy, the pipes, the pipes are calling . . .

Rose   He was called Daniel.

Shirley   What happened to him?

Rose   He went to Canada.

Shirley   Wouldn't want to go there. Too cold.

Rose   I like places like that. Remember reading all about the tundra in geography.

Charles   What's the tundra?

Rose   It's the region inside the Arctic Circle.

Charles   Tell I never listened at school, can't you?

Rose   And the Himalayas, that's another place I'd like to go.

William   She followed all that stuff about whatshisname, Hillary, in the papers. Think she wanted to go up Everest with him.

Rose   I did.

Pause.

Charles   Aren't you going to play us one of Shirley's songs, Bill?

William   I could have a go I spose.

Shirley   Play that one.

He starts to play 'How Much is that Doggy in the Window?'.

Charles   That's more like it.

Rose   Don't know it.

Shirley *sings it.*

Shirley   How much is that doggy in the window –

Charles   Woof woof.

Shirley   The one with the waggely tail?

Charles   Woof woof.

Shirley   How much is that doggy in the window?

Charles   Woof woof.

Shirley   I do hope that doggy's for sale.

Charles   Come on, Rose.

They all sing the verse again.

Shirley *does a tap dance to the tune.*

Rose   Oh, very good.

They all clap.

Rose   Time for a sandwich I think. We always have cold meat sandwich Christmas night, Shirley.

Shirley   I'll come and help you.

Charles   No, you won't. I'll help you, Mum.

Rose   Eh?

Charles What?

William *laughs*.

Rose You called me mum.

Charles I didn.

He is embarrassed.

Rose Well, come on, then. They're all done. You can carry em through.

He goes with **Rose**.

William *plays the last line of the song*.

Shirley (*sings*)   I do hope that doggy's for sale.

They laugh again.

William   I'm going to enjoy playing these.

Shirley   So why didn't you go to music college then, Mr Thorne?

William   Oh, you know how it is, dear.

Shirley   What?

William   Dad wanted me on the farm.

Shirley   Yes.

William   Probably for the best, you know.

Shirley   Mrs Youings says you play the organ like a professional.

William   Don't know about that.

Shirley   She said you've got a magic touch.

William (*he laughs*)   Oh.

Shirley   It's hard for people with artistic temperaments.

William   What?

Shirley   To fit in.

William   Maybe.

Shirley   I mean, I'm not like you. You've got a special gift.
But sometimes when I dance I feel like it's not me dancing,
it's like I'm being danced. Do you know what I mean?

William   I do. It's a form of possession you see. Some folks
might call it the work of the devil.

Shirley *shivers.*

William   You cold?

Shirley   No.

William   Come and get warm.

He takes her hand.

Freezing.

She blushes.

Shirley (*looking at his palm*)   Let me see.

William   What can you see?

Shirley (*laughing*)   A long life.

William   You look very pretty in your new dress.

Shirley   Thank you.

Charles *returns with the sandwiches.*

Charles   You two are quiet. It's Christmas, you know.

Rose *enters with the teacups.*

Rose   Hand them round.

Charles *hands out the sandwiches.*

Charles   Ummm.

Rose   What?

Charles   I haven't bought you a Christmas present,
Shirley. But there is something I'd like to give you.

Rose *shakes her head at him furiously behind everyone else's back.*

Charles   And I reckon now's as good a time as any.

He takes a small box from his pocket.

Here.

Shirley What's this?

Charles Open it.

Shirley Maybe I should save it for later.

Charles Go on.

She opens the box.

Put it on then.

He takes it from her and puts it on her.

There. You like it?

Shirley It's lovely.

Charles Rose helped me choose it.

William *looks at* **Rose**.

Charles We wondered about getting the diamond. But we decided on the sapphire in the end, didn we, Rose?

Rose Yes.

Shirley Thank you.

William Very pretty.

Rose It is.

Pause.

Want a sandwich, Bill?

William No thanks.

Rose You sure?

William I'll have one later. The pigs still have to be fed. You'll have to excuse me.

Charles There's plenty of time for that.

William Don't want to leave it too late.

Rose You want me to come?

William No. You stay here. Thanks again for the songbook. I'm going to get a lot of enjoyment out of that.

He goes.

Charles   Well, let's have some more port. Celebrate. Shirley?

Shirley   Um ...

Charles (*pouring more port into her glass*)   Here. Don't I get a kiss?

Shirley   Of course.

She kisses him.

Charles   Rose?

Rose   Not for the moment. I'll just make sure he's found the torch.

She goes. **Charles** *looks at* **Shirley**.

Shirley   It's a beautiful ring.

Charles   Yeah.

Shirley *looks towards where the other two have gone.*

Scene Six

William *is mixing food for the pigs. He has a tilley lamp.*

William   Get out! Get out.

Rose *enters with a torch.*

Rose   Thought you might need this.

William *doesn't answer.*

Rose   Luscombe's have got mains electric now, you know. In the buildings as well as in the house apparently.

No response.

Mrs Luscombe told me in church this morning.

No response.

Might be worth looking into how much it would cost.

No response.

They're fattening up. Have to get the boars done.

No response.

You gonna get the vet to do it?

No response.

I'll ring him after Christmas.

No response.

Shall I?

No response.

Bill?

William   What?

Rose   Shall we get the vet to castrate the pigs?

William   Are you going to pay him if we do?

Rose   You're not going to do it, are you? Thought you didn't like that job.

Pause.

I didn't know he was going to give her the ring tonight.

William   What are you talking about?

Rose   Charles and Shirley.

William   Doesn't bother me what he does.

Rose   Thought if I let him buy the ring it would keep him quiet for a while. Anyway he promised he'd wait till I'd talked to you.

William   Wanted to choose your moment, did you?

Rose   I thought it might all blow over.

William   Trying to handle me, were you, Rose?

Rose   No.

William   You and him think you can pull the wool over my eyes, don't you? I don't trust you, Rose.

Rose   What you mean?

William   You're sly. Always have been.

Rose   Thought you'd be pleased anyway.

William   Eh?

Rose   You're always defending her. Thought you'd like having her in the family.

Charles *appears out of the darkness.* **Rose** *shines the torch in his face.*

Rose   Nearly finished.

William *pours the food into the trough.*

Rose   You left her on her own?

Charles   She's washing up.

Rose   Charles!

Charles   I want you two to come back in there.

Rose   We're coming.

Charles   I'm going to marry her. We got to sort it out.

Rose   Not now, Charlie.

Charles   That's your solution to everything, idn it? Not now, Charlie.

Rose   It's Christmas.

Charles   Bugger Christmas. I want you two to buy me out.

Pause.

Did you hear? I want my share of the farm so I can go and get somewhere of my own. I've thought it all out. There's two ways we can do it. Either we sell off some of the land –

Rose   Charlie!

Charles   Or we get a mortgage on the farm.

Pause.

What do you say?

Rose   You want us to run up debts, Charlie?

Charles   A mortgage idn a debt. It's more like a loan.

Rose   We couldn do that.

Charles   Why not?

Rose What would father say?

Charles He idn here. He's dead.

Rose He wouldn want us running into debt.

Charles It wouldn be getting into bloody debt.

Rose Don't start swearing.

Charles It'd just be a way of getting another farm.

Rose Father didn leave us this place so we could end up
giving the money to the bank.

Charles Then we'll have to sell some of the land.
Luscombe has always wanted those fields down by the river.

Rose *looks at* **William**.

Charles Don't look to him. What do you think?

Rose Twoudn feel right.

Charles Does this feel right?

William This is our birthright. I'd rather see us dead than
sell one acre of it.

He goes.

Rose Oh, Charlie!

Charles What?

Rose How could you do this to us?

Charles Do what?

Rose We were happy. We were living together, gettin on
fine. Then you have to upset it all.

Charles Me?

Rose Rushing into things.

Charles You promised you'd speak to him.

Rose You can't wait. You want things now, today. You
don't really know anything about the girl.

Charles I know all I need to know.

Rose Hasten slowly, that's what dad would have said.

Charles Most blokes my age have been married for years.

Rose I'd've brought him round in the end.

Charles I'm marrying her. He'll have to agree in the end. It's you and me against him, Rose.

Rose Mmmm.

Charles It'll be two against one. He'll be outvoted.

Rose I suppose.

Charles Perhaps we should get some advice from Prout.

Rose Why?

Charles He was dad's solicitor.

Rose Hope it won't come to that.

Charles If it does. It does. Bill can like it or lump it.

Shirley *has entered and heard this last line.*

Shirley Mum'll be wondering where I've got to.

Charles I'll walk you home.

Shirley Night.

Rose Night.

They go. **Rose** *shines her torch on the pigs.*

Scene Seven

The yard.

Sound of pigs squealing – high-ptiched disturbing screams. **Rose** *is watching from the distance.*

William *enters.*

Rose Persuaded Charlie to do them boars while you were in town.

William Hope he's doing it properly.

Rose He did it with dad often enough. I thought you'd be pleased.

William   Is he using disinfectant?

Rose   I don't know.

William   The Dettol for it is in the barn.

Rose   Did you tell him that?

William   He hadn spoken to me for three weeks now. Since Christmas. Haven had the chance to tell him anything.

More screams.

Rose   You go and see Mr Prout?

William   Yes.

Rose   What did he say?

William   The way the will is, Charlie can't make us buy him out.

Rose   Hmmm.

William   He said it would be better to go for a mortgage rather than sell any of the land.

Rose   You don't want to do either though.

William   No.

Pause.

You think he's set on it?

Rose   He thinks he is.

William   Has he said anything to you lately?

Rose   You know Charlie. Changes with the weather.

Pause.

I don't trust Prout.

William   Why not?

Rose   He's very friendly with the bank manager.

William   Yeah.

Pause.

Those fields down by the river are boggy, mind.

Rose   So?

William   If Luscombe give us a good price.

Rose   Dad spent fifty years fighting with old Luscombe.

William   Mmmm.

Pause.

Rose   How much would the interest on the mortgage be?

William   Dunno.

Rose   Lot, I expect.

William   Yeah.

Pause.

Rose   Do you think us should speak to Luscombe about it?

William   Maybe.

Rose   Better to sell some land than get a mortgage really.

Pause.

William   Do you want to?

Rose   What?

William   Speak to Luscombe.

Rose   Do you?

William   Dunno.

Rose   Or should us go and have a chat to the bank manager?

William   What about?

Rose   A mortgage.

William   Could do.

Pause.

If you think we should give him what he wants.

Rose   You've changed your tune.

William   Who are we doing it all for?

Rose   You never wanted to be a farmer, did you?

William   Don't know what you're talking about.

Rose   Dad dedicated his life to this land.

William   I know.

Rose   Charlie can't go off on his own.

William   No?

Rose   He'd go bankrupt in no time.

William   You think?

Rose   Don't you?

William   Don't know.

Rose   Course he would. I don't know how you can consider such a thing.

William   I just thought maybe us should let him go.

Rose   And let him ruin his life? He'll soon go off her when he finds out what sort of girl she is.

William   What you mean?

Rose   Things I've heard about her. Like mother like daughter.

William   Can't always believe gossip.

Rose   You going to start defending her again, are you?

William   Don't be daft.

Rose   We should sit it out.

William   Yeah?

Rose   That's what dad would do. You know what he'd want.

William   What?

Rose   Keep the farm together. Keep the family together.

More screams from the pigs.

Rose *goes.*

The screams subside.

Charles *enters.*

William   You use disinfectant?

Charles *ignores him.*

William　Charles!

Charles *carries on walking.*

William *stops him.*

Charles　Get your hand off me.

William　I just want to know if you used Dettol. Don't want em dying of some infection.

Charles *shakes his hand off and carries on again.*

William　For Christ's sake! How much longer is this going to go on? I'm fed up with this. Bloody well ignoring me like a bloody child.

He throws his hat on the ground and stamps on it.

Rose *has heard the shouting and comes running.*

Charles　You start treatin me like a grown-up and I'll start behaving like one.

William　Don't be stupid.

Charles　You're gonna have to agree in the end. Rose and me have already talked about it.

William *looks at* **Rose**.

Charles　We can outvote you. Two to one.

William　Two to one. I see.

Charles　If you don't agree then I'm going to go and see Prout. Get him to send you a letter. Me and Rose want to sell the land down by the river to Luscombe. It's a majority decision.

William　Rose?

Charles　No use tryin to persuade her otherwise. We've agreed.

Rose　Wait, Charlie.

Charles　I'm buggered if I'm going to do any more waiting. This has gone on since Christmas. He'll have to face up to it sometime. Might as well be today.

William So? Rose? This true?

Rose You know it idn.

Charles What you mean?

Rose This is no way to settle things.

William Whose side you on, Rose?

Rose I'm not on anybody's side.

Charles She knows what's fair.

William Tell him, Rose.

Charles Tell me what?

William Rose.

Pause.

Rose dudn want to sell the land.

Charles What?

William We talked about it.

Charles You been putting pressure on her?

William No.

Charles She wants to see me settled.

William Tell him.

Rose Stop it.

William She wants to keep it all together.

Charles No.

William Ask her.

Charles Rose?

Rose Father wouldn want it. Twoudn be right, Charlie.

Charles You let him persuade you? You know why he's doin this? He's bloody jealous. The way he looks at her. Me and Shirley had a good laugh about it. Filthy bugger.

William I didn persuade Rose. She persuaded me.

Charles Don't believe you.

William   You're beaten, Charlie boy.

Rose   It's for the best, Charlie.

Charles *goes.*

Rose   Now look what you've done.

William   Eh?

Rose   That was no way to tell him.

William   You have a better way?

Rose   You should have let me do it in my own time.

William   Couldn go on like that forever. He had to know.

Charles *returns with the gun.*

Charles (*to* **William**)   I'll bloody kill you.

Rose   Charles!

William   Don't be daft.

Charles   Think I won't? You're not going to stop me marryin her. I love her.

William   Marry her. Go and work down the egg factory.

Rose   William! Charles, she idn worth it.

Charles   Don't you start.

Rose   She used to go and spend the night with Tommy Youings in the Nissan hut on the aerodrome. People saw them there together.

Charles   Bloody gossipmongers.

Rose   Mrs Luscombe's no gossipmonger. Why do you think Tommy Youings left so sudden? He skidaddled before she could get him up the altar.

Charles   Don't talk about her like that.

Rose   Nobody else would have her.

He points the gun at her.

Go on. Shoot me if you don't believe me.

Charles   Jealous, are you, Rose? Never had anything between your legs, have you? Nobody would want you.

Rose   And who'd have you? You really think any decent girl would be interested in you?

William   Rose!

Rose   You'll never amount to anything. You wouldn't survive on your own for one minute. You haven't got the staying power. You're just like Uncle Ted. And you've got his temper too. Look at you standing there pointing a gun at your own sister. Everybody in the village knows about that temper of yours. That's why Mary Quick wouldn have you. And that's why Gwen Small married the Luscombe boy. They were scared of you. You're unstable. You're nothing. You're nobody.

Charles *goes because he is about to cry.*

Rose   Don't you look at me like that.

William *goes to the pigs.*

Rose *looks after him. Pigs start screaming again.*

Scene Eight

The Ash Grove.

Charles *and* **Shirley** *are sheltering from the rain.*

Charles   We can't keep arguing about it.

Shirley   I know.

Charles   Come here.

He kisses her.

Shirley   Aowhh.

Charles   I'm sorry.

He tries to undo her clothes.

Shirley   Charles!

Charles   What?

Shirley   Don't.

Charles   What's wrong?

Shirley   Nothing.

Charles   Why don't we just get married. It'll sort itself out.

She doesn't reply.

We could go and see the vicar.

Shirley   Yes.

Charles   What about tomorrow night?

Shirley   I'm working behind the bar.

Charles   The next night then.

Shirley   I'll have to see if I'm free.

Charles   We didn't ought to wait too long.

Pause.

You been to the doctor?

Shirley   No.

Charles   But you're sure?

Shirley   Never been this late before.

He puts his arm around her.

Charles   What'll we call it?

Shirley   What?

Charles   The baby.

Shirley   I don't know.

Charles   Frances.

Shirley   Get shortened to Frank.

Charles   Not if it's a girl. That was my mother's name.

Shirley   Oh, I see.

Charles   This'll shake that old house up. Show those buggers.

Shirley   Who?

Charles   Them two. The two barreners.

Shirley   Mmmm.

He buries his head in her breasts.

Charles.

Charles   What?

Shirley   I can't live in that house.

Charles   Don't start again.

Shirley   But I can't.

Charles   We haven't got any choice.

Shirley   I don't even want to stay in this village.

Charles   Why not?

Shirley   Because of the way people look at me. The way they look down on mum.

Charles   You don't want to listen to drunks gossiping in the Red Lion.

Shirley   It's not just them though, is it?

Charles   What you mean?

Shirley   It's Rose and William.

Charles   What about them.

Shirley   I can't live with them.

Pause.

We don't have to stay here, do we?

Charles (*violently*)   This is what they want!

Shirley   What?

Charles   They want me to move out. Then they can have the farm to themselves. Do what they like with it.

Shirley   Let them.

Charles   Why should they get it their way? It's mine as much as theirs.

Shirley   You'll get your share one day.

Charles   Yes. And in the meantime I have to go and slave
my guts out for somebody else! They're not getting rid of me
that easy. I'm not going to be somebody else's wage slave just
to suit them.

Shirley   But I can't live in that house with them.

Charles   They'll soon get used to it.

Shirley   But I won't. It wouldn't work out, Charles. We
could go to Australia with mum and Mr Webber. There's all
sorts of opportunities out there.

He takes her face in his hands and speaks into it.

Charles   Now listen to me! We're getting married and
we're living here. There's no argument. That's what's going
to happen.

He releases her.

She takes the ring off.

Shirley   Here.

Charles   Don't be bloody daft!

Shirley   Take it!

Charles   Put it back on.

She looks at him. He kisses her.

You have to be kept on a tight lead I can see that.

Shirley   What you mean?

Charles   You're too wilful. I'll have to break you in.

He tries to undo her clothes.

Come on.

Shirley   You're hurting me.

Charles   Come on!

Shirley (*violently*)   No!

He looks at her.

I'm not a bloody pony you bought at Bampton Fair you
know.

Charles I'm sorry.

She puts her head in her hands.

Shirley.

Shirley It'll never work, Charles.

Charles We'll make it work.

Shirley When I was a kid I used to lie in bed listening to my mum and dad rowing in the next room. We lived with my gran and grandad – my dad's parents. My gran always looked down on my mum. So then mum used to go and complain to dad about her and they'd end up rowing. Mum always says if they'd had a house of their own they'd still be together now. That'll happen to us, Charles.

Charles Bit late for second thoughts now, idn it?

Shirley What you mean?

Charles You're carrying my kid.

Pause.

Shirley And what if it idn yours?

Charles Eh?

Silence.

Shirley What if the baby looks like Tommy Youings when it's born?

Charles Will he?

Shirley I don't know. But all the old hens in the village will be clucking over it and nudging each other. (*She mimics them sounding like a hen.*) 'Awwwhhhh, dudn look much like Charlie Thorne to me.'

Charles *says nothing.*

Shirley Mr Webber will find you a job in Australia, you know. He's got relations over there.

No response.

Charles?

Charles What?

Shirley   I do love you.

She holds up the ring.

It's up to you.

Charles *looks at her.*

Suddenly he grabs the ring and goes.

Shirley *cries.*

Scene Nine

William *is playing the piano.*

Sound of knocking.

Rose (*off*)   Charlie! Charlie!

Pause.

(*Off.*)   Charlie, come on, you've got to eat.

William *stops playing and listens.*

Rose (*off*)   Charlie, please. It's dumplings.

Pause.

Rose *enters with a tray.*

William   Has he eaten anything?

Rose   Don't think he's touched it.

William   He'll have to eat it in the end.

Rose   You eat that chutney in the larder?

William   What chutney?

Rose   The chutney we had with the pie yesterday.

William   No.

Rose   He must have been down in the night and had it.

William   Why?

Rose   Because it's all gone.

William   Whole jar of chutney?

Rose Yes.

Pause.

It's been going on for nearly a month now.

William Mmmm.

Rose You think we ought to get the doctor for him?

William What can the doctor do?

Rose I'm worried, Bill.

William No point being worried.

Rose I'd hate to see him . . .

William What?

Rose Always remember when they took Mrs Warren's sister down Digby.

William Charlie won't end up in no lunatic asylum.

He plays. She listens.

Rose We'll be all right, won't we, the three of us?

William Course we will.

Rose *starts humming the tune.*

Rose They're leaving next week.

William Who?

Rose Mr Webber, Mrs Stephens, Shirley.

William Oh.

Rose They're going to Sydney. That's where his folks are.

William *plays the piano.*

William (*sings*) Within the woodlands, flowry gladed
  By the oak trees' mossy moot
  The singing grass blades, timber-shaded,
  Now do quiver underfoot;
  And birds do whistle overhead
  And water's bubbling in its bed

Rose *joins in.*

Both   And there, for me, the apple tree
   Do lean down low in Linden Lea.

William *starts the next verse with* **Rose** *accompanying him with her humming*.

William   When leaves that lately were aspringing,
   Now do fade within the copse
   And painted birds do hush their singing
   Up upon the timber tops;

Both   And brown-leaved fruit's aturning red
   In cloudless sunshine overhead,
   With fruit for me, the apple tree
   Do lean down low . . .

They notice **Charles** *standing in the doorway. He has just a pair of long johns on*.

Rose   You'll catch your death.

William   Get his night-shirt.

Rose *goes*.

Charles (*sings tunelessly*)   Three German officers crossed the line
   Parlez-vous
   Three German officers crossed the line
   Parlez-vous

William   Stop that, Charlie.

Charles   Three German officers crossed the line
   Kissing the girls and shagging the wives

William   Stop it.

Rose *returns with the night-shirt*.

Rose   Here you are, Charlie.

He continues singing and runs away from her.

Charles   Inky pinky parlez-vous.

Rose   Stop mucking around, Charlie.

William   Give it to me.

He approaches **Charles**. **Charles** *runs away again.*

William   Don't be so bloody daft.

Charles *turns round and moons at them.*

They chase him round the room. Every time he escapes he cocks a snoop at them. He continues singing the song.

Eventually they corner him. **William** *tackles him and pins him to the ground.*

William   Give me the shirt.

Rose *and* **William** *struggle to get the shirt on him.*

William   Pull it down.

Even though he is trapped **Charles** *continues singing.*

Stop singing that.

Charles *sings louder.*

William   Stop it. You should be ashamed of yourself singing that in front of your sister.

Charles *carries on singing.*

William *covers* **Charles**'*s mouth.* **Charles** *moves his head aside and carries on.*

William   You want me to get dad's horsewhip?

Rose   Bill, don't.

Charles *carries on singing.*

William *gets a horsewhip.*

William   You want this?

Charles *stops singing.*

William   You want it?

Charles (*sings mock sweetly*)   Oh, don't deceive me,
Oh, never leave me.
How could you treat a poor maiden so?

They look at each other as the lights fade.

Part Two

Scene Ten

It is thirty years later. An exposed field in winter.

William *has been pulling mangolds. He carries a sack and puts it down. Coughs. Blows into his hands. Coughs again. He is an old man and frail.*

Rose *enters. She is arthritic.*

Rose   Wondered where you'd got to.

William   Getting some mangolds pulled.

Rose   Go back home, Snowy. Go on, my lovely. She's followed me all the way up here.

William   Bloody cat thinks it's a dog.

He coughs.

Rose   You shouldn't be out in this wind.

William   Had to be done.

Rose   You taken your medicine this morning?

William   Forgot.

Rose   Brought your gloves.

She hands them to him.

William   Ground's frozen solid.

Rose   Snowed last night on the moors.

They stand looking into the distance. Two forlorn figures on a frozen landscape.

In the distance a tractor can be heard. They look in that direction.

Walter Luscombe's out on his new tractor.

William   Where?

Rose *points. They watch.*

Rose   Got his little boy with him.

She sings quietly to herself.

We plough the fields and scatter the good seed on the
land . . .

William   Dunno how they afford all that machinery.

Rose   Letter came this morning from the bank.

William *doesn't respond.*

Rose   You want to read it?

William   Haven't got my glasses.

Rose   You ask the bank manager if he could wait for the
interest payment?

William   Yes.

Rose   What will we do if he won't?

William   Mmm. Here! Charlie! Charlie! Bag em up!

Rose (*sings*)   He sends the snow in winter
The warmth to swell the grain . . .

He's building his parents a bungalow.

William   Who?

Rose   Walter Luscombe.

William   Look at him! What's he doing?

Rose   We could sell some land.

William   Still have to farm the rest.

Rose   Charlie will have to do more of the heavy work.

William   Charlie! What can he do? Any job I give him I
have to stand over him.

Rose   He's not that bad.

William   He can't be relied on.

Rose   So what should we do?

William   We'll have to think of something.

He coughs.

Rose   He's going to put central heating in.

William   What?

Rose   Walter Luscombe. In this bungalow.

William   Ohhh.

Rose   Mornacott Cottage is coming up for sale.

No response.

If we sold the farm we could easy afford that even after paying off the bank.

Still no response.

It'd be big enough for the three of us. And it's got a field, we could keep a few hens and pigs. Charlie would be pleased. He hates the work.

William   I'm not living in a bloody cottage in the village.

Rose (*sings*)   All good gifts around us
Are sent from Heaven above
Then thank the Lord
Oh, thank the Lord
For –

William   You read the letter?

Rose   No. You want me to?

William (*calling to* **Charles**)   Come on, get on with it!

Rose   If they won't let us have any more we'll have to do something.

William *coughs*.

Rose   Look at you! Out pulling mangolds with that cough.

William   We can't afford to buy cow cake.

Rose   And we can't carry on like this. I need some money for the baker.

William   Haven't got any.

Rose   He comes today.

William   Have to pay him out your egg money.

Rose (*sings*)   Much more to us, His children
He gives our daily bread.
All good gifts around us
Are sent from Heaven above . . .

William *opens the letter*.

Rose   I was going to use the egg money for my trip.

William   What trip?

Rose   With the church. To Oberammergau.

William   Have to pay the interest to the bank.

Rose   That heifer will be calving soon. You can sell the calf to do that.

William   Won't be worth selling till spring.

William *is trying to read the letter*.

Charles *enters with a sack of mangolds and some of the green tops in his hand*.

William   You need to take them down and give them to the bullocks.

Charles *stands looking at Walter Luscombe on his tractor*.

William   What you looking at?

Rose   That's Walter Luscombe.

Charles   Big tractor.

Rose   Yes, it's new.

Charles   Bout time we had a new tractor.

William   Get those bullocks fed.

Charles (*quietly*)   Bugger off.

Rose   Charles!

William   What did you say? What did he say?

They don't answer.

What you doing with those greens?

Charles   Feed my rabbits.

William   Bloody rabbits. We're supposed to be farmers.

Rose   Leave him.

William   Dad must be turning in his grave. Waste of bloody time.

Charles (*mimicking their father*)   'We're not bloody townies, we don't have bloody pets.'

Rose   Charles.

Charles   'If you want to keep a pet go and live in a rabbit hutch in Exeter.'

Rose *starts to giggle*.

William   Don't encourage him.

Charles   'And you should have got these mangolds pulled out before Christmas. Not wait till they get frozen in.' Look, there he is over there behind the hedge. He's watching you, Billy.

Rose *find this hysterically funny and tries to stifle her giggles*.

William   You'll end up back in that hospital if you say things like that.

Rose   Shut up, Bill. Take the mangolds down and feed the cows, Charlie.

Charles *picks up the sack and goes*.

They stand watching him.

Rose   Sometimes I think I see mum. I was looking out the kitchen window the other day and it was like I saw her in the lane out the corner of my eye. In that blue dress of hers. Funny.

William   You're both mad.

He is trying to read the letter.

Rose   Here.

She reads it.

William   Well?

Rose   Dear Mr Thorne, as you are aware, the interest payments on your loan are now over a year in arrears. I'm afraid we are unable to offer you any further extension and would ask you to pay the outstanding amount as promptly as possible. Yours faithfully, D.W. Lambert.

They stand watching Walter Luscombe on his tractor.

Look at Snowy. She's waiting for me to walk home with her. I'm coming, my lovely.

(*Sings.*) All good gifts around us
Are sent from Heaven above ...

You want your dinner, don't you?

William   Take some mangolds down with you.

Rose   What are we going to do?

William   I don't know.

He goes to pull some more mangolds.

Rose *picks up the sack.*

Scene Eleven

The yard.

Charles *is standing with a fork looking at the sky. The rooks are gathering in the elms.*

Charles   Caw, caw, caw.

Rose *enters.*

Rose (*sings*)   Blessed assurance, Jesus is mine:
Oh what a foretaste of glory divine!

Chick chick, chick. Cubby, cubby, cubby. Chick, chick, chick. There you are, my darlings. There's some scraps for you. What you doing, Charlie?

Charles *doesn't respond.*

Rose   I thought you were going to muck out the pigs.

He still doesn't respond.

Don't let Bill catch you standing around.

Charles   There was rooks in the wood down Digby.

Rose   Yeah?

He goes.

You want something too, Snowy? Do you, my lovely?

She goes and gets a milk jug.

(*Sings.*) Heir of salvation, purchase of God;
   Born of his spirit, washed in his blood,
   This is my story, this is my song
   Praising my Saviour, all the day long . . .

There you are, my lovely. My pretty little darling. Yes. You
wanted that, didn't you?

(*Sings.*) This is my story, this is my song,
   Praising my Saviour all the day long.

William *enters.*

Rose   You get back indoors. You shouldn't be up. Doctor
said you had to stay in bed. (*To the cat.*) Yes, is that a nice
drink of milk? Do you like that, my lovely? Lap, lap, lap.
Lap, lap, lap. My pretty little Snowy.

William   Has Charlie mended that gap in the hedge?

Rose   I don't know. Look at you. If you don't shift that
cough off your chest you'll get pneumonia.

(*Sings.*) Perfect submission, perfect delight.
   Visions of rapture burst on my sight . . .

William   Cows'll be gettin into Luscombe's winter kale
again.

Rose (*sings*)   Angels descending, bring from above
   Echoes of mercy, whispers of love.

William   I'll go and have a look at that heifer later.

Rose   No you won't. I'll do that. (*To the cat.*) You finished
already, my lovely?

(*Sings.*) This is my story, this is my song.
   Praising my Saviour all the day long.

William   Letter came from the solicitor.

Rose   What?

William   Forms to sign.

Rose   What forms?

William   For the auctioneer.

Rose   Oh.

William   What?

Rose   Didn know you'd already asked him to do that.

William   I hubm asked him to do anything.

Rose (*sings*)   This is my story, this is my song,
   Praising my Saviour, all the day long.

William   He just said he'd send me the forms in case we decided to sell up.

Rose   All right, all right. No need to start shouting about it.

William   We don't have to sign em if we don't want to.

Rose (*sings*)   Perfect submission, all is at rest,
   I and my Saviour am happy and blest.

Pause.

Who has to sign them?

William   All three of us, I spose.

Rose (*sings*)   Watching and waiting, looking above,
   Filled with his goodness . . .

William   Anybody'd think I was going behind your back.

Rose (*sings*)   . . . lost in His love.

William   You're the one who wants to go and live in the village.

Rose   Just said it might be easier.

William   You want to go off gallivanting with the church group. Spending all the egg money on a ticket to bloody Austria. But you don't want to give up anything.

Rose   That egg money's mine. I don't sit in the pannier market all day Thursdays just to end up spending that money on you two.

William   You eat the bread too.

Rose   I've sacrificed everything all my life and the one time I want to do anything, go somewhere, you tell me I can't. I could have grandchildren by now if it wadn for you two.

William   Why didn you marry bloody Danny Marks then?

Rose   Because I couldn leave you and Charlie. That's why.

William   We've all made sacrifices.

Rose   You going to start talking about music college again? I didn't stop you going to music college. All our lives you've talked about how dad stopped you going to music college. It's a tune you've played for the last fifty years. I'd've thought you'd've got tired of it by now. I am.

William   And I'm sick and tired of hearing you talk about spending money we haven't got.

Rose   Whose fault's that?

William   What you mean?

Rose   We wouldn't be in debt if you hadn borrowed that money from the bank.

William   You bloody old fool. I only did it because of you. Going on about how we needed a new milking parlour.

Rose   You can't have my egg money.

William   We'll sell the bloody farm then.

Rose   Sell it for all I care. I don't want to stay living here with a nincompoop and an old miser.

Charles *crosses.*

William   You mended that gap in the hedge?

Charles   I'm cleaning out the pigs.

William   Have a look at that heifer.

Charles *goes.*

Rose He'll have to agree, you know.

William He'll bloody well do what we tell him.

Rose I'll have a word with him.

William He won't bloody care.

He goes.

Rose (*sings*) This is my story, this is my song . . .

A car drives up.

Rose *looks.*

Sound of car door slamming.

Shirley *enters. She is tanned and looks young for a woman in her early fifties.*

Rose You lost?

Shirley No.

Rose Thought you might be looking for Luscombe's.

Shirley No, Rose. I was looking for you.

Rose Sorry, my dear, do I know you?

Shirley Don't you recognise me, Rose?

Rose Now you do look familiar. You're the old vicar's daughter, aren't you?

Shirley No.

Rose Well, let me see . . .

Shirley It's me, Rose.

Rose Yes.

Shirley *laughs.*

Rose I know the face.

Shirley Shirley.

Rose Shirley? Oh my . . . No! Oh, so it is! Who'd have thought! Oh, I knew I recognised the face. But I just didn . . .

Shirley Haven't got that old, have I?

Rose   Old? No. You don't look old. You don't look old at
all. It's just, well . . . look at you!

She laughs.

Shirley Stephens. Well I never.

Shirley   Thought it was about time to come back and visit
the old country.

Rose   Yes.

Shirley   When I arrived in London everything seemed to
have changed so much. But the closer I got to here the more
familiar it all started looking.

Rose   You driven all the way?

Shirley   From Australia?

Rose   No, from London. From Australia! That's a good
one! Have to tell Bill that one.

Shirley   Be a long drive.

Rose   Yes. That's right. It would.

Shirley   I got a train to Exeter and hired a car.

Rose   Oh yes. Goodness. So have you been here long?

Shirley   You remember my uncle, Mr Curtis? He used to
be a car breaker.

Rose   Oh yes, he moved up to Essex, didn he?

Shirley   That's right. I've been staying with him for a
couple of weeks.

Rose   He's still alive then?

Shirley   Oh yes. And Mr Thorne?

Rose   What?

Shirley   Is he well?

Rose   Bill?

Shirley   Yes.

Rose   Well, we're all getting older.

Shirley   Yes.

Rose   Where are you staying?

Shirley   I was going to try the Red Lion.

Rose   The Inn Place it's called now.

Shirley   Yes?

Rose   You can't stay there.

Shirley   Why not?

Rose   It's a terrible place. The police are always getting called there.

Shirley   Oh dear. I'll need to find somewhere.

Rose   Yes.

William *comes to see who has driven up*.

Rose   Look who it is, Bill.

Shirley   Hello, Mr Thorne.

William   How do.

Shirley   I knew you'd recognise me.

William   Oh yes.

Rose   Who is it, then?

William   Ummmm.

Rose   See, I knew he didn't. It's Shirley.

William   Ahhhh.

Rose   Shirley Stephens.

William   Oh!

Rose   Come all the way from Australia.

William   I knew I knew you.

Rose   That's what I said.

Shirley   How are you, Mr Thorne?

William   I can't complain.

Rose   Got a terrible chest.

Shirley   Oh dear.

William We're all getting older.

Shirley Yes. Thirty years, you know.

Rose No.

Shirley It is.

Rose Never believe it. Hear that, Bill? Thirty years since she was here.

William Your mother well?

Shirley She died.

William Oh, I'm sorry.

Shirley In seventy-eight. And Mr Webber, you remember him?

William Course we do.

Shirley He died last year. He never got over mum's death.

Rose Sad.

Shirley They had some good years. They ran a roadhouse up near Alice Springs.

Rose Fancy.

Shirley That building wasn't here before, was it?

Rose No. We built that a few years after you went to Australia. It's a milking parlour.

Shirley Thought I didn't recognise it.

Pause.

Rose She's looking for somewhere to stay, Bill.

William The Luscombe's do bed and breakfast.

Rose Oh, I don't think ...

Shirley No.

Rose There's a new place at Haddon Cross. It's a motel.

Shirley Is it expensive?

Rose I don't know.

Shirley Perhaps I could phone them.

Rose We're not on the phone, dear.

Shirley Oh.

Rose We're backward.

She laughs.

Shirley Don't expect you miss it.

Rose Don't have telly either.

William Nearest phone is down at the crossroads.

Shirley Right.

William You over here on your own then?

Shirley My son came with me.

William Oh.

Shirley He's stayed in Essex with my uncle.

William Doesn't he want to see where you used to live?

Shirley I might bring him down here later. We're here for a month.

Rose And your husband?

Shirley Pardon?

Rose He not with you?

Shirley No. I uhh, I'm not married.

Pause.

I've got some photos in the car of mum and Mr Webber and places we lived.

William We'd like to see them, wouldn we, Rose?

Rose Yes.

William Kettle on?

Rose She doesn't want to be too late getting to the motel. They say it's going to snow.

Shirley Oh dear.

Rose I've got their number written down cause they buy their eggs off us sometimes. I'll just go and see if I can find it.

She goes.

Shirley *gets out a cigarette.*

Shirley   Would you like one?

William   No thanks. Never smoked.

Shirley   Of course. It's probably these things that killed
mum. But I need one after that drive. I learnt to drive in the
outback where you can see anything come for miles. Not used
to those hedges.

The rooks caw. They look up.

I'd forgotten about the rooks.

William   Oh yes.

Shirley   Your brother . . . Charles . . . used to shoot them.

William   They can be pests.

Shirley   Yes. Is he . . . ?

William   Don't know where he is. Might be down over
mending a hedge.

Shirley   Oh. Is he well?

William   Oh, he's all right, yes. He's very well. We're still
going down the same old track. Just the ruts have got deeper.

They laugh.

Shirley   Just the three of you?

William   Eh?

Shirley   I just wondered if . . .

William   No, we all stayed single.

Pause.

Shirley   I often used to think about you.

William   Ahhh.

Rose *returns.*

Rose   There you are.

She hands **Shirley** *a piece of paper.*

Shirley   Thank you.

William   Sure you haven't got time for a cup of tea?

Shirley   Rose is right, I'd better check in.

William   But you'll come back?

Shirley   All right.

Rose   Tonight?

Shirley   Or tomorrow.

Rose   Roads will be treacherous.

Shirley *looks at her watch.*

Shirley   I expect you go to bed early.

William   No, no. You come back later. We want to see your photos.

Rose   She'll have to drive all the way back in the dark.

Shirley   I don't want to put you out.

William   We'll save you some food.

Shirley   Thank you.

Charles *enters. He stops.*

Shirley   Good evening.

Charles   Yes.

Rose   Do your trousers up. How many times do I have to tell you?

She goes and pulls up his zip.

Shirley (*she still hasn't recognised* **Charles**)   So where is this motel?

William   Don't you remember Haddon Cross?

Shirley   Ummm...

William   Other side of the old aerodrome.

Shirley   Oh, yes.

Charles   That heifer looks like calvin.

William   Shouldn be due yet.

Charles   Her's springin. Got her tail in the air.

Rose   Why haven't you started the engine?

He doesn't answer. They all look at him.

Charles.

Shirley *gasps.*

Rose   It's getting dark. I need some light in the kitchen.

Charles *goes.*

Shirley *looks at them.*

Shirley   I didn't recognise him.

William   No.

Rose   Is there diesel in the engine?

Shirley   Is he ... he seemed so ...

Sound of engine starting.

Rose   That's our generator. Got electric now.

Shirley   Yes.

Rose   Tidn mains. But it's good enough for us. Better get that supper on.

William   We're having stew. You like stew, Shirley?

Shirley   Maybe I should leave it for tonight.

William   No, my dear, you come back. Us'll have a good chinwag.

Shirley   I see. Right. Well. I'll see you later.

William   See you later.

Shirley   Bye.

She goes.

Rose   Drive careful.

Shirley (*off*)   I will.

She goes.

The car starts. **William** *and* **Rose** *wave. Headlights cross them.*

William Bye.

They stop waving.

Rose What do you think she wants?

William Eh?

Rose Must be after something.

William Don't be daft.

Rose Coming back here after all these years.

William Speck she wants to show her son where she was brought up.

Rose He's not with her though, is he?

Charles *crosses.*

William He didn't even recognise her.

Rose Don't you believe it.

Pause.

Don't stay out here getting cold.

She follows **Charles**.

Scene Twelve

The parlour.

Shirley, **William** *and* **Rose** *are laughing. They have been drinking* **Shirley**'s *duty-free Baileys.*

Shirley And do you remember old Bert who used to come round the village with the baker's van?

William Oh, yes, Bert Gibson. Come from Crediton way.

Shirley He only had one arm.

Rose That was from the Great War.

Shirley 'Want any cakes today, missus?'

Rose/Shirley 'Fresh out the oven.'

They laugh.

Rose He was our mother's fourth cousin, twice removed.

Shirley Really?

Rose Yes, I found that out when I was looking into our family history.

Shirley Oh.

William Don't start going on about that.

Rose Why not?

William Get her started on family history and you'll never stop her.

Shirley I used to be scared of him.

Rose He was harmless.

Shirley Oh, Rose!

She laughs.

Rose What?

Shirley Can you hear what you just said?

William Ah, that's right. That's right.

Rose What did I say?

William and **Shirley** *are laughing.*

Shirley You said he was armless.

Rose Eh? Oh, that's terrible. Oh no! Oh!

She laughs.

That's a good one, Bill. Armless! Oh!

They all laugh.

She was only a baker's daughter but how she kneaded the dough!

William Yeah.

Shirley What?

Rose That was one of dad's jokes.

Shirley Oh, yeah. Here, have some more.

Rose Oh, no. I mustn't, dear. You'll get me drunk.

Shirley *pours some more Baileys in her glass.* **Rose** *gets some papers.*

Rose   Here, what do you think of this, Shirley?

Shirley   What is it?

William   Oh my God!

Rose   You be quiet. She'll be interested in this. It's our family tree. I've traced dad's family back to the sixteenth century and mum's back even further.

William   The hours she spends on it.

Rose   I went through all the church records.

William   Spent a fortune writing off to Somerset House in London.

Shirley   It's amazing.

Rose   See this is Bert Gibson's family over here.

William   He's dead now, you know.

Rose   Went out delivering in the rain on the Wednesday. Got pneumonia. Died on the Friday.

Shirley   Oh dear.

Rose   Yes.

Shirley *starts laughing.*

Rose   You're terrible.

They all laugh.

Twadn the cough that carried him off, twas the coffin they carried him off in.

Shirley   Yes, yes.

Rose   That was another of dad's.

The laughter subsides.

Shirley   You still play the organ at church, Mr Thorne?

Rose   No, he doesn't. He doesn't go to church any more.

Shirley   Oh.

Rose   Says he's an atheist.

Shirley   Don't you play at all?

William   No, my dear.

Shirley   That's a shame.

William   I've forgotten.

Rose   Course you haven.

William   What do you know about it?

Rose   All right. All right. See what he gets like, Shirley?
Number of times I ask him. He never will.

Shirley   Not even for me, Mr Thorne?

William   I'm too rusty my dear.

Shirley   This will oil you up.

She pours some more drink in his glass.

Rose   That's a good one.

Shirley   We won't mind if you play a few wrong notes.

William   Oh, I don't know.

Shirley   Just for me?

William *hesitates.*

Rose   Go on.

They clear the piano.

William   What shall I play?

Rose   I don't know.

He starts playing 'Waltzing Matilda'.

William (*sings*)   Once a jolly swagman camped by a
    billabong
    Under the shade of a . . .

Shirley   Koolaba tree.

Shirley/William   And he sang as he watched and waited
    while his billy boiled

You'll come a-waltzing Matilda with me.
Waltzing Matilda, waltzing Matilda *etc*.

They laugh.

Rose Oh, look at Snowy. She wants to join in. Go on, nosy parker, you know you're not allowed in here.

Shirley Hello, there, puss.

Rose Go on.

She giggles.

That's my little baby.

Shirley She's lovely.

Rose Yes.

William Give us a song then, Rose.

Rose I'm not singing.

William Come on, give us 'The Ash Grove'. You know that one, Shirley?

Shirley I can't remember.

William There, she can't remember it. So you gotta sing it to her.

Rose I can't.

Shirley I remember you having a lovely voice.

Rose Not any more.

William *starts to play*.

William (*sings*) Down yonder green valley
Where streamlets meander . . .

How does it go?

He begins playing the song from the beginning.

Rose *sings*.

Shirley *is thoughtful*.

Charles *enters. He and* **Shirley** *look at one another. Suddenly the others notice him standing at the doorway with his hot water bottle in his hand.* **Rose** *stops singing*.

Rose   There you are. Thought you were going to stay out there all night with those rabbits.

Charles   Want to fill my bottle.

Rose   Put the kettle on and I'll come and do it.

Charles   Snowing.

Rose   Is it?

Charles   Settling too.

Shirley   Would you like some of this, Charles?

Charles   No thank you.

He goes.

Rose   He's been out feeding his rabbits.

William   Where's these photos you were going to show us?

Shirley   Oh yes.

Rose   You won't be able to see anything without your glasses.

William   I can see.

Rose   What's the point of having them if you never wear them? He's vain, that's what it is, Shirley.

Shirley *gets the photos.*

Shirley   That's mum and Mr Webber outside the roadhouse.

Rose   It's like a hotel, is it?

Shirley   Yes. Right out in the bush. Our nearest neighbour was forty miles away.

Rose   Goodness me. Look, Bill.

Shirley   That was a party we had for mum's seventieth birthday.

Rose   Lot of people.

Shirley   And that was a holiday we went on to the Snowy Mountains in Victoria.

Rose   Fancy that. Never think of Australia having snow.

Shirley Oh yes.

Rose They very high mountains?

Shirley Only about four thousand feet.

William Thinking of going over there and doing a bit of skiing, are you, Rose?

Shirley People do.

William Imagine Rose trying to walk up there with her arthritis.

He laughs.

Rose He never thinks I can do anything, Shirley.

William Tidn true.

Rose I wanted to go to Austria next year but he won't let me.

William I'm not stopping you.

Rose Says we can't afford it. Never afford anything.

William Wants to go and see the Passion Play with the church.

Shirley Oh.

Rose What's wrong with that?

William Nothing.

Rose Just because you've stopped believing.

William What good's going to church ever done you?

Rose Hear that, Shirley? If mum could hear you running down the church.

William Pah.

Rose And dad wouldn't like it.

William He didn go from one year to the next.

Rose He believed in God.

Shirley These are some of Francis. My son. This was one Christmas on the beach when he was ten.

William   Oh yes.

Rose   Let me see.

He hands it to her.

Rose *gasps.*

William   What?

Rose   Nothing. Come on, show me the rest.

Shirley   This is him when he was fifteen with some friends of mine.

Rose   Where was that taken?

Shirley   In a hotel in Sydney. I was working there as a dancer. Those are other women in the troupe.

Rose   You kept up your dancing then.

Shirley   Yes. That's Frank in his car. He'd just got it. And this is one of me and him and his girlfriend, Laura.

Rose   Yes.

Shirley   They're getting engaged when we get back.

William   You look more like sisters.

Shirley   Oh, Mr Thorne, you're such a gentleman.

William   You do.

Shirley   She's a lovely girl.

William   You both are.

Charles *enters.*

Charles   Kettle's nearly boiling.

Rose   All right.

Charles *goes.* **Rose** *follows him.*

William *is looking at the photo of Francis.*

Shirley *looks at the picture of their father on the wall.*

Shirley   He was a handsome man.

William   Yeah.

Shirley   How old was he there?

William   Late twenties?

Shirley   Same age as Frank.

William   He had a temper mind.

Shirley   Yes?

William   When I was a boy I climbed the apple tree in me best trousers and tore em. He took me out in the barn and whipped me with the horsewhip.

Shirley   That's terrible.

William   That's what parents were like in those days.

Shirley   How old were you?

William   Eight or nine.

Shirley   It's barbaric.

William   I deserved it I expect.

Shirley   Well . . .

William   He was preparing us for a hard life.

Shirley   Farming?

William   Yes.

Shirley   But you wanted to go to music college, didn't you?

William   You get daft ideas when you're young.

Shirley   You don't regret not going?

William   No point regretting anything, is it?

Shirley   No.

William   You can't escape your fate.

Shirley   What?

William   That's what I've come to believe, Shirley. Some people are born to happiness. Some aren't.

Shirley   Maybe.

William   You was one that was born to happiness.

Shirley   Was I?

William   Bet you haven't got many regrets.

Shirley   It's not all been plain sailing, Mr Thorne.

William   No?

Shirley   It was hard work. Specially when Frank was small. It was just me and him. We were on the road a lot. But there were compensations.

William   Yeah?

Shirley   The girls, all the other dancers, got on well. It was like being in a family really. Frank had lots of aunties.

William   Ahhhhh.

Rose *enters*.

Rose   He says that heifer's not looking too good.

William   What's wrong with it?

Rose   Just lying there, he says.

William   Better get out and have a look.

Rose   You wrap up, it's snowing.

Shirley   I should be going.

William   You stay there. We won't be a minute.

Rose *and* **William** *go*.

Shirley *walks to the photo of the father on the wall. She has a photo of Frank. She covers the bottom half of the face and compares the eyes on the two photos.*

Charles *appears in the doorway.*

Charles   I knew you as soon as I saw ee.

Shirley   Did you?

Charles   Yeah. Never forget a face.

Shirley   It's a long time.

Charles   They say you been living in Australia all this time.

Shirley   That's right.

Charles   I know a bloke who went to Australia.

Shirley   Really?

Charles   Archie.

Shirley   Oh yes.

Charles   Archie Blackmore. He lives near Perth.

Shirley   That's Western Australia.

Charles   Went out there sheep-shearing.

Shirley   I see.

Charles   Tall bloke. Bit cross-eyed.

Shirley   Ah.

Charles   You never come across him?

Shirley   Uh, it's a big country.

Charles   Might be dead by now. Fair few years ago.

Pause.

Shirley   You sure you wouldn't like some of this?

Charles   What is it?

Shirley   It's whiskey and cream.

Charles   Whiskey and cream in a bottle?

Shirley   Yes.

Charles   Caw!

Shirley   Would you like some?

Charles   Don't know.

Shirley   Here.

She pours him a glass.

He smells it.

Tastes nice. Honestly.

He tastes it tentatively.

Well?

Charles   Yeah.

She smiles.

They tell you about me rabbits?

Shirley   Your rabbits?

Charles   Yeah, I breed em.

Shirley   Oh.

Charles   Won a prize at the Flower Show with me chinchilla.

Shirley   That's good.

Charles   I got quite few rosettes.

Shirley   Great.

Charles   Thing about showing rabbits is you gotta look after em. Keep em clean.

Shirley   I'm sure.

Charles   Then you have to shampoo em before the show.

Shirley   Really?

Charles   Yeah, it's quite an art mind.

Pause.

What's the photos?

Shirley   Pictures of Australia. My mum.

Charles   Can I have some more of that drink?

Shirley   Help yourself.

Charles   Funny stuff, idn it?

Shirley   Would you like to see them?

Charles   What?

Shirley   The photos.

Charles   I'm not one for looking at photos.

Shirley   This is my son. Francis.

She hands him a photo.

Charles *looks at it.*

Charles   Yeah, I won second prize for me chinchilla and got a special commendation for me New Zealand white.

Shirley   Great.

Rose *enters.*

Rose   Thought you'd gone to bed.

Charles   I'm on me way.

Rose   How many of those have you had?

Charles   This is my first.

Rose   Did you ask?

Charles   Course I bloody asked. You bloody fool.

Rose   That's enough of that.

He finishes his drink and leaves the room.

Tidn good for him to get drunk.

Shirley   Oh, I don't think –

Rose   He started going down the pub a few years ago. I had to put a stop to it.

Shirley   I see.

Rose   It's his temperament you see.

Shirley   Yes?

Rose   Always been highly strung. They had to give him that electric shock treatment when he was in the hospital. Depressed, you see, so they had to shake him out of it.

Shirley   When was that?

Rose   Back in fifty-five.

Shirley   I see.

Pause.

Rose   Good job he didn't have children, isn't it?

Shirley   How do you mean?

Rose   Might have passed it on.

William *returns. He has snow in his hair.*

Rose   Look at you, I told you to put your hat on.

William *doesn't respond.*

Rose   Well?

William   Don't know.

Rose   Gonna be all right though, idn it?

William (*snaps*)   I don't know.

Pause.

Shirley   I ought to be going.

William   Hope you can get through to Haddon Cross.

Rose   The grit lorry will have been out.

William   Not on the road down to the village.

Shirley   I'll be all right.

William   We could light a fire in the back bedroom, put you up for the night.

Shirley   It's OK.

Rose   I'll show you out. Where did you leave the torch, Bill?

William   Kitchen table.

Shirley   It's OK.

Rose   It's dark out in that yard. Don't want you slipping up. Anyway I gotta come and switch off the generator.

She goes.

Shirley   Well . . .

William   Yes.

Shirley   It's been lovely to see you again, Mr Thorne.

William   And you, my dear. And you.

Shirley   I'm going to take a look round the village tomorrow.

William   Come up and see us.

Shirley   All right. Night, then.

He plays the piano.

William   Good night, Irene, good night, Irene.
   I'll see you in my dreams.

She kisses him on the cheek.

Rose *enters with an unlit candle and the torch.*

Rose   Here's your candle.

Shirley *and* **Rose** *go.*

William *plays the piano – something classical he learnt as a boy.*

The lights go off. (**Rose** *has turned off the generator.*)

William *continues playing.*

Rose *returns with her own candle.*

Rose   Haven't you lit it?

She lights **William**'s *candle.*

She goes and gets **William**'s *medicine and pours it out in a spoon.*

Rose   Here.

He opens his mouth and she gives it to him.

Get the vet in the morning for that heifer.

William *doesn't respond.*

Rose   Come on.

She hands him his candle.

William *stops playing, closes the piano and takes the candle.*

William   She's left one of her photos.

He picks up the photo of Frank. He starts to get his glasses out.

Suddenly **Rose** *snatches the photo from him.*

Rose   No.

William   What?

Rose   I know what you're thinking.

William   I'm not thinking anything.

Rose   Nice little trap she's laid and you're falling straight in it.

William   Don't be daft.

Rose I'm not the one that's daft. He could be anybody's kid.

William You can see the likeness then, can you?

Rose You never saw her for what she was.

William What you mean?

Rose She's a scheming bitch.

William Rose.

Rose I've got a long memory, William Thorne. I remember how you looked at her that Christmas Charles brought her here. And I saw the very same look in your eyes tonight. When was the last time you played the piano for anybody? 'Irene, good night, Irene.' I heard you. And I saw your eye wandering all over her body.

William You're bloody mad.

Rose She's pulled the wool over your eyes good and proper.

William There's no wool over my eyes.

Rose Well, if there idn, let's get that paper signed and this farm sold so we don't get into any more debt. Then we can go and live in a bit of comfort in our last few years.

William I don't mind signing the forms.

Rose So why haven't you? And now you're going to have second thoughts, aren't you? Think you might be able to leave it to that boy, do you? Just cause that tramp can wind you round her little finger. It's disgusting. An old man like you!

William *goes and gets the papers.*

William Get me the pen!

Rose *hesitates.*

William Go on! What you waiting for?

Rose *still doesn't move.*

William There's usually one in here on the mantelpiece. Where's the bloody pen, woman?

Rose Keep your voice down.

William You're telling me I'm wavering about selling this place. Just give me the pen and I'll sign it.

Rose That one doesn't write.

William Well, find me one that does. Go on! Where do you keep your pen? In here? No. In here? Ahhhh, here we are. Now hold the candle so I can see.

Rose William, you'll tear it.

William Hold it!

He takes her wrist and brings it close in order to illuminate the paper.

Rose You're hurting me.

He signs the paper.

William Now you.

Rose What's the point?

William Eh?

Rose We've still got to get Charles's signature.

William Soon do that. Come on! Sign!

She hesitates.

Ahhhhh! Scared, are you? Take the pen!

Rose I'm not doing it tonight like this.

William *throws the paper at her.*

Knock at the door.

Shirley (*off*) Hello? Haven't gone to bed, have you?

Rose *goes through to the kitchen.*

Shirley *enters the kitchen.*

Shirley Got stuck in the lane.

Rose Oh dear.

Shirley I don't think I'll be able to get out tonight.

William (*from the parlour*)   Get that fire lit in the back bedroom, Rose.

Rose *smiles at* **Shirley**.

Scene Thirteen

The kitchen.

The Baileys has been put on the mantelpiece together with the paper from the auctioneers. **Charles** *enters and helps himself to the Baileys. He sees the papers and reads them. He hears someone coming and hides with the Baileys.*

Rose *enters. Sits. She is crying and wipes her eyes.*

William *enters with a half-plucked white chicken.* **Rose** *blows her nose.*

William   I've already done some of it.

Rose   It's old, this one. Be tough.

She starts plucking the chicken.

How long do you think it had been dead?

William   The calf?

Rose   Yes.

William   Week or so.

Rose   Least we've got it out now.

William   Ahhh.

Rose   Will the heifer be all right?

William *doesn't answer.*

Rose   She doesn't look too good. Better call the vet.

William *stares into space.*

Rose (*sings*)   Breathe on me breath of God,
  Fill me with life anew –

William   Where's Shirley?

Rose   How do I know?

William   All right.

Rose   Shirley this. Shirley that. I'm fed up with it. Going and pulling the neck of one of my best layers just so Shirley can have chicken for dinner. You should be thinking about how we're going to pay the interest at the bank now we've lost that calf.

William   Thought you wanted to sell up. All you gotta do, Rose, is sign that bit of paper.

Rose *doesn't answer*.

William   It's there.

No response.

You know what dad would want.

Rose   What?

William   If there was someone to pass it on to.

Rose *says nothing*.

William   If dad thought he had a grandson to carry on farming the place then he'd want him to have it.

No response.

Wouldn't he?

Rose   He's a gyppo.

William   Then sign that bit of paper if that's what you feel. You want to cut your nose off to spite your face then do it, Rose.

He goes.

Rose *wipes her eyes*.

Rose (*sings*)   Breathe on me breath of God.
  Until my heart is pure.
  Until with Thee I will one will
  To do and to endure.

Shirley *enters*.

Rose   Just picking this hen. William's pulled its neck in your honour. Said we ought to have something special for dinner.

Shirley   You don't have to worry about me.

Beat.

How's the calf?

Rose   Dead.

Shirley   Oh no.

Rose   Been dead a week, Bill reckons. He's worried about the heifer. Thinks it might not survive.

Shirley   You called the vet?

Rose   Not yet.

Pause.

Shirley   The car won't start.

Rose   No?

Shirley   I went down to the phone box.

Rose   Oh yes?

Shirley   To talk to the car hire people. I have to phone them back tomorrow morning. They can't get out here until the roads are cleared.

Pause.

Always remember plucking the geese and turkeys for Christmas.

Rose   Yes.

Shirley   You used to have about ten women doing it, didn't you? Everyone laughing and joking.

Rose   We haven't done that for years. Can't compete. All factory farming now. We been left behind.

Rose *cries.*

Shirley   You all right?

Rose   This hen's old. Have to boil it.

Shirley   You all right, Rose?

Rose   We were banking on that calf. We got interest to pay at the bank.

Shirley   Did you borrow money?

Rose   We had a run of bad luck. The milk marketing people wouldn't take our milk because we weren't on mains. So we borrowed some money from the bank to get mains laid on and build a new milking parlour. Then the very next year we had an outbreak of foot and mouth. All the cattle had to be slaughtered and burnt. We never recovered our losses. So we still owe the bank and we could never afford to build up the herd again. Hasn't been used for years that milking parlour. Just sits there. Don't know what dad would say.

Shirley   You did your best.

Rose   It wadn good enough.

She cries.

Shirley   Rose. Rose.

Rose   It's all we know, this place. It's all we know.

Rose *sobs.* **Shirley** *holds her.*

William *enters.*

William (*not unkindly*)   Look at you, you silly old thing.

Rose   Leave me alone.

She goes.

Shirley *gets up to follow her.*

William   You'd better leave her.

Pause.

Shirley   I'm sorry about the calf.

William   It's the heifer I'm worried about.

Shirley *nods.*

Shirley   What are you going to do?

William   Rose had some daft idea about us moving into Mornacott Cottage. We'd spend the rest of our lives looking out the window at the churchyard waiting for the day when they take us in there and bury us.

Shirley   Is it a lot of money you owe?

William   Well, no, it idn really.

Pause.

I went up the attic this morning.

Shirley   Oh yes?

William   Found this.

Shirley   What is it?

He gives her the ring.

William   It's been up there in an old tea box for years. Sort of thing you come across when you're looking for a collar-stud or a button. Thought you should have it.

Shirley   But it's his.

William   He hasn't looked at it for years. Probably thinks it's lost. Your son could give it to his girlfriend. As an engagement ring.

Shirley   I couldn't.

William   He won't miss it.

She holds the ring.

Shirley   You know, don't you?

William   What?

Shirley   About Frank. Who his father is.

William   Yes.

Rose *enters. They look at her.*

Shirley   I wasn't sure to begin with. But as he got older he got more and more like Charles.

William   Looks like our dad.

Shirley   I thought that.

William   What does he do?

Shirley   He works night shift in a car factory. But he doesn't like it. He wants a change. But he hasn't got any qualifications, you see. That's my fault. We travelled around so much. So his schoolwork suffered. I can't help him out. I

was never one for saving money. And I can't dance any
more. When Mr Webber died he left us a few hundred dollars
so we thought we'd make this trip.

William   Come and look us up?

Shirley   Yes.

Pause.

William   You think he'd make a farmer?

Shirley   He's a good boy. Hard-working.

Rose *is listening. Picking the hen.*

William   We haven't got anybody else to leave the farm to.
Our branch of the tree hadn got any more shoots on it, has it,
Rose?

Rose   I need some logs for the Rayburn.

William   All right.

Shirley   I'll help you.

William   No need.

He goes, whistling 'Waltzing Matilda'.

Shirley   You going to burn off the little hairs?

Rose   Yes.

Shirley   Where do you keep the matches?

Rose   Mantelpiece.

Shirley   Newspaper?

Rose   In the porch.

They leave.

Charles *emerges from his hiding place.*

In the yard **William** *is watching* **Rose** *and* **Shirley** *try to light the
newspaper in order to burn the hairs off the chicken.*

Shirley   I'll hold the chicken, Rose. You light the paper.

Rose   Mind you don't set fire to yourself.

William   You want me to do it?

Rose No. You go and put those logs in the fire. Here,
Shirley.

Shirley *screams*. **Rose** *and* **William** *laugh*.

Scene Fourteen

The rabbit shed. Rosettes are pinned up.

Charles *is looking into his rabbit hutch and stroking the rabbit
inside.*

Rose *enters*.

Rose The dinner's nearly ready.

No answer.

Charles.

No response.

Aren't you coming in for your dinner?

Still no response.

I gave them some cabbage leaves this afternoon.

No response.

Rose Is that the one that won the rosette at the show?

Charles This is Esau.

Rose Is he the one?

Charles What?

Rose The one that got the prize?

Charles That was his father, Isaac.

Rose Don't know what the vicar would say about you
giving them names from the Bible.

Charles He's got more fur, that's why.

Rose That's why what?

Charles That's why he's called Esau.

Rose What you mean?

Charles Esau was a hairy man.

Rose That's right, he was.

Pause.

Got to talk to you, Charlie.

Charles I'm feeding me rabbits.

Rose It's important though.

Charles How much longer is she staying?

Rose Who?

Charles Her.

Rose Shirley?

Charles Yes.

Rose She's waiting for them to bring her another car from Exeter.

Charles Mmm.

Rose Charles, we been talking.

Charles Who?

Rose Me and Bill.

Charles What about?

Rose Bout the farm. Bout how it's too much for us. If something doesn't happen soon we're going to lose the place.

Pause.

Need someone young to help us.

Charles Stephen Warren.

Rose Eh?

Charles He's young. He used to work for Luscombes but they don't need him no more because Michael Luscombe's left school.

Rose We can't afford to pay wages. We need someone young to pass the farm onto.

Charles We haven't got anybody.

William *enters*.

William   You give that heifer any water?

Rose   I haven't.

William (*to* **Charles**)   Have you?

Charles *picks up the rabbit's bowl and goes*.

William   Hasn't touched any of the cake we gave her.

Pause.

Sittin out here with the rabbits when we got a heifer that might die.

Rose   I was trying to get him to come in for his dinner.

William   Let him starve if he wants to.

He sees the photo in her hands.

What's that?

Rose   I thought I'd try and talk to him.

William   What about?

Rose   This boy. Frank, whatever his name is.

William   No point talking to him about it.

Rose   He'd have to want it.

William   Don't be so bloody daft. What's the point of talking to him? You drive me bloody mad.

Rose   We couldn't just go ahead without getting Charles to agree.

William   Course he's going to agree. It's his son, isn't it?

Charles *returns with water for the rabbits*.

William   Here, Charlie.

Charles *ignores him*.

William   We got some news for you.

No response.

Now listen. You got a son. In Australia.

Rose   Bill!

William   He's going to come over here and help us run this place, see.

Rose   Stop it, Bill. Let me talk to him.

They look at **Charles** *who is still busy with his rabbits.*

Charles.

No response.

Charles. He's a nice-looking boy.

William *grabs the photo from* **Rose**'s *hand.*

William   Here, Charlie. Look at this.

Charles   I don't want to see it.

William   Don't be so bloody daft. See, this is what you get for trying to talk to him.

Shirley (*off*)   Hello! Where are you?

They look at each other.

(*Off.*) Hello? Rose? Mr Thorne?

William   Here we are, Shirley.

Charles   I haven't got a son.

William   You have. Shut up!

Shirley *enters.*

Shirley   The potatoes are done.

Rose   We're coming.

Shirley   Oh, are these your rabbits?

Charles *doesn't answer.*

Shirley   Isn't he magnificent?

Rose   That's Esau because he's hairy.

Rose *laughs.*

Shirley   Pardon?

Rose   Don't you remember the story of Jacob and Esau?

Shirley   Oh yes.

Charles I want my ring back.

Rose What ring? What are you talking about?

Charles He gave her my ring.

Rose What's he talking about, Bill?

Charles Give it back to me.

William You shut your mouth.

Charles Come on.

Shirley It's indoors.

Charles I want it back.

William You watch yourself. We'll get you committed. The doctor will send you back to that mental hospital.

Charles Give me back my ring. I know what you're up to. All of you. You didn't want it thirty years ago so you can't have it now. Give it back.

William (*to* **Rose**) This is your bloody fault. Coming out here talking to him as if he was normal. He's your son, you daft bugger.

Charles I haven got a son.

William Course you have.

Charles Her's lying.

Shirley Charles?

Charles What?

Shirley Please.

Charles Please? Please what? Please yourself. That's what you did. With whoever you wanted. Except me. We never did it. So he can't be mine. He's Tommy Youings' son. That's who's son he is. Not mine. Everybody knew she was a bloody whore.

William *struggles with him.*

Rose Bill.

Charles *throws him off.*

Shirley He's your son, Charles.

Charles Give me back my ring.

Shirley *goes.*

Charles He idn my son.

William He's doing this to spite us.

Charles You'll never know, will you?

He goes.

William There's tests they can do.

Rose We can't force him to make the farm over.

William We can get the doctor to say he idn fit though.

Rose No.

William What?

Rose I'm not going to make him do anything.

Pause.

Perhaps this is our retribution.

William What's that supposed to mean?

Rose For what we did to him.

William We didn't do anything to him.

Rose Don't get yourself worked up.

William You're enough to try the patience of a bloody saint.

Rose It wouldn be right to do anything against his wishes.

She goes. **William** *throws his hat on the floor and stamps on it.*

Scene Fifteen

The Ash Grove.

Shirley *is standing, looking.*

William *enters.*

William Ahhhh.

Shirley You shouldn't come out here with your cough.

William I'm all right.

Shirley Why aren't you with the vet?

William I know what he's going to say.

Rooks. They look up.

They always gather here before they go and roost over in the rookery.

Pause.

Look . . .

Shirley Yes.

William Bring him here.

Shirley No.

William They'd have to come round in the end.

Pause.

Shirley This is where it happened, you know. What he said didn't happen.

William Covered in bluebells in the spring.

Shirley I remember.

William The Venus of the Woods.

Shirley Pardon.

William That's what they call the ash.

Shirley Oh.

William Very useful wood, ash.

Shirley Yes.

William Used to make all the implements out of ash.

Shirley Really?

William Not any more.

Pause.

Wouldn't he like to be given the chance?

Shirley   What?

William   Your boy. To run this place.

Shirley   No, Mr Thorne.

William   Why not?

Shirley   This is no life for him. He's an Australian. He belongs in the sun. I don't want him to – I think it would be hard for him.

William   With Charlie?

Shirley   Yes.

Pause.

He'll be all right. He'll find his way.

William   Dad used to keep the Ash Grove immaculate. Every year we used to come out and harvest a few trees. You had to thin em out see. They can't grow properly if they're too close.

Rose (*off*)   William!

Shirley *goes to move.* **William** *puts his finger over his lips.*

Rose   William!

William   You think you'll ever come back?

Shirley   No, probably not. I shouldn't have come this time. You can't go back.

William   That was your fate, you see, to leave.

Shirley   Maybe.

William   And this farm was ours. Now it's draggin us back into the earth.

Shirley   You mustn't give up.

William   I sit out here sometimes. Think about the world. How it's changed in my lifetime. But things don't get better, do they?

Shirley   Don't they?

William   Bombs. Wars. Just gets worse.

Shirley   Maybe.

William   Only comfort I can find is that it's probably all happened before and will happen again. Endless circles going round and round. A world comes into being. People evolve. Civilisation. Then we destroy it all, blow it all up. And it all starts up again.

Shirley *says nothing*.

William   Stands to reason.

Shirley   You don't have to think like that, you know.

William   People invent reasons for carrying on, like Rose with her family tree and her church and her God. But they're just deluding themselves.

Shirley   There's always hope.

William   Hope?

Shirley   Anything could be round the corner.

William (*holding up his palm*)   What does it say here?

She smiles.

Too late for me to turn any corners.

Shirley   My mum always said it's never too late to start again.

Pause.

William   I'll see him all right, your son. Once we get this place sold. He can expect a little windfall.

Shirley   You don't have to.

William   I want to.

Rose *enters with the gun*.

Rose   There you are.

William   What do you want?

Rose   The vet was going to put that heifer down but I said we'd see to that. Are you going to do it or shall I?

William I'll do it.

William *goes*.

Rose You see the man from the car hire?

Shirley Yes.

Rose He says the plugs are damp. He's trying to fix it.

Shirley I'm ready when he is.

Rose You be careful on those roads. They're still icy.

Shirley I will.

Rose You going back to Essex?

Shirley Yes.

Rose To your uncle.

Shirley Yes. He's going to come to Australia for the wedding.

Rose Old Mr Curtis?

Shirley Yes.

Rose Fancy him going all that way at his age.

Gunshot.

Oh dear.

Shirley It's a shame.

Charles *enters*.

Rose Go on, Charles.

Charles *starts to go*.

Shirley Here.

She takes out the ring.

Take it. He shouldn't have given it to me. It's yours.

Charles Thank you.

Shirley I'm leaving, Charles. I won't be back again.

Pause.

William *returns*.

William   That bloke's got your car going.

Shirley   Right, well.

Rose   Mind that black ice.

Shirley   I will.

She goes to kiss **Rose**. **Rose** *puts her hand out.*

Goodbye, Charles. Good luck with your rabbits.

Charles   Thank you.

William *and* **Shirley** *go.*

Charles *looks at the ring.*

Sound of car starting.

Rose   It's started this time.

Sound of car departing.

She has the auctioneers' papers in her pocket.

Charlie?

Charles   What?

Rose   We got these papers from the auctioneers.

Charles   Oh yes?

Rose   It's to let him put the farm up for sale.

Charles   I see.

William *returns.*

Rose   We'll all have to sign it.

Charles   Then what'll us do?

Rose   We can go and live in Mornacott Cottage. Look, I've signed it.

Charles   I'm not signing anything.

Rose   Charles.

Charles   You didn't want to sell it thirty years ago. I don't want to sell it now.

Rose   We'll end up losing everything.

Charles You can't make me. This is our home.

Rose *looks at* **William**. **William** *ignores her.*

Rose The vet said he can't come again unless we pay him.

William *doesn't respond.*

Rooks. They look up.

Rose Those rooks make such a racket.

Charles You got any money?

Rose What for?

Charles I want to go to Hatherleigh. There's a rabbit breeder going to be at the market.

Rose You should save your money.

Charles I don't get paid.

Rose I haven't got any.

Charles Can't you let me have some of the egg money?

Rose We need that.

Charles Just a couple of quid.

Rose This is the last time mind.

She gets her purse.

Charles Look at him looking at me. Begrudge it to me, do you, you old miser?

Rose Charles!

Charles He thought he'd found somebody to hand it all on to. You hadn't though, had you, you daft old bugger!

Rose Here take it.

Charles *goes.*

Rooks. They look up.

Rose There's Snowy. Hello, my darling, I'm coming. (*To* **William**.) Don't stay out here getting cold.

She goes.

William *looks up at the birds. He takes aim and shoots.*

He reloads.

Rose *comes running back. The rooks are taking flight.*

Pause.

Charles *comes to see what is happening.*

All three look at each other.

William *holds the gun.*

Blackout.

Sound of three gunshots.

Lights up.

A white cat runs onto the stage and picks its way amongst the bodies. The lights fade.

Methuen Modern Plays

include work by

Jean Anouilh
John Arden
Margaretta D'Arcy
Peter Barnes
Sebastian Barry
Brendan Behan
Edward Bond
Bertolt Brecht
Howard Brenton
Simon Burke
Jim Cartwright
Caryl Churchill
Noël Coward
Sarah Daniels
Nick Dear
Shelagh Delaney
David Edgar
Dario Fo
Michael Frayn
John Godber
Paul Godfrey
John Guare
Peter Handke
Jonathan Harvey
Iain Heggie
Declan Hughes
Terry Johnson
Barrie Keeffe
Stephen Lowe

Doug Lucie
John McGrath
David Mamet
Patrick Marber
Arthur Miller
Mtwa, Ngema & Simon
Tom Murphy
Phyllis Nagy
Peter Nichols
Joseph O'Connor
Joe Orton
Louise Page
Joe Penhall
Luigi Pirandello
Stephen Poliakoff
Franca Rame
Philip Ridley
David Rudkin
Willy Russell
Jean-Paul Sartre
Sam Shepard
Wole Soyinka
C. P. Taylor
Theatre de Complicite
Theatre Workshop
Sue Townsend
Judy Upton
Timberlake Wertenbaker
Victoria Wood

Methuen World Classics

Aeschylus (two volumes)
Jean Anouilh
John Arden (two volumes)
Arden & D'Arcy
Aristophanes (two volumes)
Aristophanes & Menander
Peter Barnes (two volumes)
Brendan Behan
Aphra Behn
Edward Bond (four volumes)
Bertolt Brecht
  (five volumes)
Howard Brenton
  (two volumes)
Büchner
Bulgakov
Calderón
Anton Chekhov
Caryl Churchill
  (two volumes)
Noël Coward (five volumes)
Sarah Daniels (two volumes)
Eduardo De Filippo
David Edgar (three volumes)
Euripides (three volumes)
Dario Fo (two volumes)
Michael Frayn (two volumes)
Max Frisch
Gorky
Harley Granville Barker
  (two volumes)
Henrik Ibsen (six volumes)

Terry Johnson
Lorca (three volumes)
David Mamet
Marivaux
Mustapha Matura
David Mercer (two volumes)
Arthur Miller
  (five volumes)
Anthony Minghella
Molière
Tom Murphy
  (three volumes)
Musset
Peter Nichols (two volumes)
Clifford Odets
Joe Orton
Louise Page
A. W. Pinero
Luigi Pirandello
Stephen Poliakoff
  (two volumes)
Terence Rattigan
Ntozake Shange
Sophocles (two volumes)
Wole Soyinka
David Storey (two volumes)
August Strindberg
  (three volumes)
J. M. Synge
Ramón del Valle-Inclán
Frank Wedekind
Oscar Wilde

For a Complete Catalogue of Methuen Drama titles
write to:

Methuen Drama
Michelin House
81 Fulham Road
London SW3 6RB